English Sketches

Sketches from the English Teaching Theatre

intermediate

2

Doug Case
Ken Wilson

MACMILLAN
HEINEMANN
English Language Teaching

Macmillan Education
Between Towns Road, Oxford OX4 3PP
A division of Macmillan Publishers Limted

Companies and representatives throughout the world

ISBN 0 435 26397 8

Text © Doug Case and Ken Wilson 1995
Design and illustration © MacMillan Publishers Limited 1998
Heinemann is a registered trademark of Reed Educational and Professional Publishing Limited

Designed by Kevin McGeoghegan MCSD

Cover design by Keith Shaw at Threefold Design

Cover photograph by Chris Kelly, showing Garry Fox and Angela Marshall in the
'Tourist Information' sketch.

Acknowledgements

As in the original editions of both *Off-Stage!* and *Further Off-Stage!*, we would like to
express our thanks to these people:

- to John Haycraft, for having the original idea for the ETT, and for constant support
  and encouragement ever since;
- to Jeremy Harrison and Piers Plowright, who first gave the ETT a style and identity;
- to all the members of the ETT, past and present, who have performed with us on
  our tours;
- to all the organizations who have helped us with our tours, particularly
  International House and the British Council;
- and, most of all, to all the teachers and students who have been our audiences,
  organizers and hosts, for their help, kindness, hospitality and enthusiasm.

Doug Case and Ken Wilson
April 1995

Printed in Great Britain by Athenæum Press Ltd, Gateshead, Tyne & Wear

2003 2002
11 10 9 8 7 6 5

Contents

Teacher's introduction

Structural levels chart

Index of language areas

Sketches

1 Gerry Thatcher's party
2 The army
3 The dentist
4 Mr Williams and the postman
5 Tourist information
6 The bank
7 The Superlative vacuum cleaner
8 Superman and the psychiatrist
9 The lost property office
10 The travel agency
11 Gerry Brown's driving test
12 Giovanni's café
13 Shakespeare's house
14 Mr Universe
15 The new James Bond film
16 World record

Teacher's introduction

English Sketches 1 and 2 are a set of Teacher's Resource Books at two levels: Elementary (Book 1), and Intermediate (Book 2). Each book contains sixteen sketches, which can be used by secondary school students and adult learners, in class or in other contexts such as English clubs and end-of-term shows. An audio cassette or compact disc containing recordings of the sketches accompanies each book.

The sketches in these Teacher's Resource Books comprise twenty-three of the sketches which first appeared in *Off-Stage!* and *Further Off-Stage!*, originally published by Heinemann in 1979 and 1984 respectively, together with nine new sketches. All the sketches are taken from shows performed by the English Teaching Theatre between 1974 and 1994.

The English Teaching Theatre

The English Teaching Theatre (ETT) is a theatre company which produces stage shows for learners of English all over the world. The shows consist of sketches, songs and other activities, all involving a lot of audience participation, and are designed to be enjoyed by both teenagers and adults; the format evolved from a style of teaching in which the use of sketches, songs and role-playing is considered very useful. ETT performances take place in schools, in adult education centres and in many other settings, such as teacher-training institutes, language schools and theatres.

The ETT was originally the idea of John Haycraft, the former Principal of International House, London, a private language school with branches and affiliates all over the world. In 1969, John said to one of his teachers, Jeremy Harrison: 'Why don't we have a theatre specially for students of English?'

From 1970 to 1972, the ETT idea was developed in a series of summer season performances in London. Then, in 1973, the British Council invited the group to tour Germany, and the touring side of the ETT's work began. Since then, the group has undertaken over 170 tours, visiting more than 40 countries around the world; these countries include most of Western Europe, seven countries in Latin and South America, seven in West Africa, four in the Middle East, Uzbekistan and Japan.

The usefulness of sketches

John Haycraft's summary of the usefulness of the ETT applies equally well to the use of sketches in general: 'It makes students aware that English is not just words, structures and idioms, but that it is a lively, dramatic and versatile means of communication. It emphasizes too, that learning and teaching can and should be pleasurable.'

Sketches can, of course, be used simply as entertaining material for listening or reading. Above all, however, they provide enjoyable *speaking* practice, whether they are re-enacted by the students with their scripts in their hands, used as a basis for improvisation, or learnt for a more elaborate performance. They require attention to stress, intonation and overall clarity: if the 'audience' can't hear the words clearly, they won't be able to appreciate the jokes! Depending on the context in which the sketches are being used, the 'audience' may simply be other students in the class, or an actual audience. Whatever the context, working on sketches is a collaborative activity and can have benefits for general student interaction as well as for language practice.

Choosing sketches from
English Sketches 1 and 2

Above all, we hope that you will be choosing a sketch to do with your students because you believe that they will find it funny and enjoyable.

All the sketches in *English Sketches* 1 and 2 can be used at a variety of levels. Even if a sketch is designated as 'elementary', its humour can make it enjoyable for intermediate or more advanced students; conversely, even a sketch designated as 'intermediate' may be useable with elementary students, because its situation is clear and accessible – and once again because of the humour.

The language used in the sketches is controlled but not artificial. As a reviewer of one of the original books, *Off-Stage!*, remarked, to our great pleasure: 'The material covers a fairly standard progression of structures and functions, but the sketches are not so crammed with obvious and repeated grammar points as to be in any way tedious. Quite the reverse, in fact: while many teaching texts set out to be funny, the English Teaching Theatre actually succeeds in making students laugh' (Ben Duncan, *ARELS Journal*).

You will naturally be choosing sketches which are generally appropriate to your students' level, and also perhaps because they help to reinforce the practice of particular language areas from the course you are using. You could thus select a sketch according to its structural level, its subject matter, the situation in which it takes place, the functions expressed by the characters or the attitudes the characters adopt, for example. To help you in your selection, this book contains:

- A *Structural levels chart*, which provides a general guide to the structural levels of the sketches.

- An *Index of language areas*, which is an alphabetical list of functions, notions, topics and situations occurring in the sketches.

Using sketches from *English Sketches* 1 and 2

Each sketch has an introductory page of accompanying notes, arranged as follows:

- Brief comments on the background to the sketch.

- **Words and expressions:** some words and expressions occurring in the sketch which you may wish to teach or revise before working with the sketch itself. You may not wish to deal with them *all* beforehand, however, as the students can deduce many meanings in context (and, in some cases, focusing on the words beforehand may spoil the surprise of a joke).

- **Preliminary practice:** ideas for an activity to introduce the sketch. These are usually short oral activities, involving mime, questions and answers, and so on.

- **Follow-up activities:** ideas for activities to use after working with the sketch itself. These are usually further role-playing activities developed from the situation of the sketch.

- **Props and costumes:** notes on props and costumes needed for both a simple classroom re-enacting of the sketch and for a more elaborate performance. For re-enacting in the classroom, these are always simple and easily obtainable objects.

Here are some suggestions as to how you could use the sketches, firstly *in the classroom* (or an English club, for example), where the ultimate aim is not to perform for an outside audience, and secondly *for a performance*.

In the classroom

Having chosen a sketch which you feel is appropriate, you could of course simply play the recording straight through allowing the students to listen, and then move on to the printed script. It is helpful, however, to add other activities to this rather 'bald' approach. Here is a possible sequence.

1 Teach or revise some words and expressions from the sketch as you feel necessary.

2 Do the suggested preliminary practice.

3 Give the students two or three pre-questions, i.e. questions about the sketch for which they will find the answers while listening to the audio-recording. (If it is not possible for you to use the audio-recording, see the *Note* at the end of this section.)

4 Play the audio-recording, perhaps stopping occasionally for predictions (e.g. when a character asks a question, invite the students to guess what the response will be).

5 Follow up on the pre-questions.

6 Play the audio-recording a second time, doing some intensive work on short sections from the sketch (e.g. a few lines of dialogue which include strongly stressed words or special intonation) and/or stopping the recording periodically for students to supply succeeding lines from memory.

7 Distribute photocopies of the script, and move on to the students' re-enacting of the sketch. In small classes, the students can practise the sketch in groups, with each group having the right number of characters for the sketch. They then act out their versions for the rest of the class; if time is short, one group could begin this acting out, then hand over to another group who continue from the point the first group reached, and so on until the sketch has been performed.

In large classes, this re-enacting could be done as follows. Put the students into groups. These groups will contain more students than there are characters in the sketch, but all the students should have something to do, so the groups should be encouraged to add extra characters (even if they only say one line each). The students practise in their groups, and then act out their versions for the rest of the class.

Of course, for these re-enactings in class, it is perfectly all right for the students to have their scripts in their hands – and indeed this is what we would recommend. When the students are familiar with a particular sketch, they may like to try re-enacting it in a freer way, 'in their own words', perhaps based on key words from the different parts of the sketch (written on cue-cards or on the board).

Where necessary, in any re-enacting, male characters can be played by female students, and vice-versa.

8 Finally, you might like to do some of the follow-up activities.

Note: If you are working without the audio-recording, you could start with the printed script of the sketch. Photocopy it and remove some of the words, with Tippex for example; then photocopy this modified version and distribute it to the students, who give their ideas for the missing words. (This idea could also be used when you have the audio-recording: while listening, the students jot down the missing words in the spaces as they hear them. There should only be *short* omissions, and the students can use their own shorthand abbreviations if they like.)

For a performance

Of course, a 'performance' might just be an informal re-enacting, with scripts, in front of other members of the class, or students from other classes. In this case, arrange for the groups to rehearse in private, so that their preparations are not overheard by their 'audience'.

When preparing for a more elaborate performance, such as an end-of-term show, many of the ideas given above for class work will be useful, but there will be other considerations too.

You and the students will need to decide how many sketches are to be performed, who is going to perform them (the less keen 'actors' could have small parts), what else the show might contain – and also what any non-performers are going to do: e.g. they could deliver 'links' in the show (short introductions to the sketches) and help with the preparation of props and costumes. Rehearsals may take place over a fairly lengthy period, when time allows in class or outside class. Of course, the students will actually

have to *learn* the scripts, paying particular attention to clarity, stress and intonation: the audio-recordings will be a useful guide.

The preparation involved in working towards such a performance can be time-consuming, but it and the performance itself can make for an immensely rewarding experience, and contribute greatly to the students' confidence in and enjoyment of English.

And finally…

At the back of this book you will find a few pages headed 'Notes and reminders'. You may like to use these pages in two ways:

- You could use them for your own notes – which sketches worked particularly well with which type of class, useful variations you discovered on the activities suggested, etc.

- When the students are preparing for a performance such as an end-of-term show, you could photocopy them for use as sheets to give to the students, with notes and reminders about rehearsal times, props and costumes which need to be prepared, who is to learn which parts, etc.

Whatever the context in which you use the sketches, we hope that you and your students enjoy working with them, and that the audience, if there is one, enjoys watching them.

Structural levels chart

Although the sketches in Book 1 are designated as *elementary* and those in Book 2 as *intermediate*, all can be used at a variety of levels. As a general guide to the structural levels, the following chart shows the principal verb forms (tenses and related structures) which occur in the sketches.

Book 1

#		Present Simple	Present Continuous	Past Simple	Future: *going to*	Future: *will*	Present Perfect	Present Perf. Cont.	Past Continuous	Modal aux. +past part
1	Tea break	●								
2	The ticket inspector	●	●	○	○					
3	The King of Boonland	●	●							
4	The restaurant	●	●							
5	The doctor	●	●		○	○	○			
6	Gussett and Rose	●	●	●				○	○	
7	The passport office	●	●	●						
8	Fire practice	●	●	●						
9	The post office	● §	● +	●	○					
10	Mr Jones	●	●	●				○		
11	The shoe stall	● §	●	●			○	○		
12	The check-in desk	●	●	●	○	○	○			
13	The police	● §	●	●				○		
14	Hotel Splendido	● +	● +	●	○	○	○			
15	The bus stop	●	●	●	●	●				
16	A ticket to Birmingham	+ ● §	+ ● §	● O	●	●				

Book 2

#		Present Simple	Present Continuous	Past Simple	Future: *going to*	Future: *will*	Present Perfect	Present Perf. Cont.	Past Continuous	Modal aux. +past part
1	Gerry Thatcher's party	● +	● +	●	●	●		○		
2	The army	● §	●	●	●	●		○		
3	The dentist	●	●	●	●	●	●			
4	Mr Williams and the postman	●	●	●						○
5	Tourist information	●	●	●	●	●				
6	The bank	● §	● §	●	●	●				
7	The Superlative vacuum cleaner	●	●	●	●	●				
8	Superman and the psychiatrist	●	●	●	●	●			○	
9	The lost property office	● §	● §	●	●	●	●			
10	The travel agency	●	●	●	●	●	●			
11	Gerry Brown's driving test	●	●	●	●	●			○	○
12	Giovanni's café	●	●	●	●	●	●			
13	Shakespeare's house	●	●	●	●	●			○	
14	Mr Universe	●	●	●	●	●	●	○		
15	The new James Bond film	●	●	●	●	●		○		
16	World record	●	●	●	●	●	●	●		

● = Occurring freely in sketch. ○ = Occurring in sketch in only one or two instances, which can be treated 'idiomatically'.

+ = Including for 'future arrangements'. § = Including in conditionals or after time conjunctions. O = Including in conditionals.

Index of language areas

This Index lists the main 'language areas' – notions, functions, topics and situations – occurring in the sketches in both Book 1 and Book 2. (The verb forms noted in the Structural levels chart, like other structural points, are only listed here if there are particularly salient occurrences in a given sketch.)

References are given to the book and the sketch. For example, **1** 1 = Book 1, Sketch 1; **2** 8 = Book 2, Sketch 8; etc.

Ability **2** 8
Adjectives, Superlative **2** 7
Advice **1** 16, **2** 8, 10
Airports **1** 12, **2** 5
Army **2** 2
Asking for information **2** 5
Asking someone out **2** 1
Banks **2** 6
Booking
– a holiday **2** 10
– a hotel room **1** 14
Buses **1** 15
Buying and selling **1** 11, **2** 7, 13
can/can't, could(n't) (ability) **2** 8
can't/must (deduction) **2** 13
Cars, Renting **2** 5
Checking in
– at a hotel **1** 14
– at an airport **1** 12
Clothes **1** 11, 13, 14
Comparisons (more/less than, twice/half as much as) **2** 6
Complaining **1** 11, 14
Confusions over words **1** 5, 9, 12, 13, 15, **2** 1, 5, 6, 15
Contradicting and correcting **1** 1, 5, 6, **2** 1, 6
Countries **1** 3, 9, 12, **2** 5, 10
Country, Talking about your **1** 3
Currency **1** 3
Deductions (can't/must) **2** 13
Dentists **2** 3
Describing people and things **2** 7, 8, 9
Doctors **1** 5
Driving **2** 11
Explanations and instructions **1** 1, 8, 13, **2** 2, 6, 11
Feelings **1** 11
Film stars **2** 15
Fire station **1** 8
Food and drink **1** 1, 4
Going out **1** 4, **2** 1
Hobbies **1** 6, **2** 14
Holidays **2** 10, 12
Hotels **1** 14
Illness **1** 5
Imperatives **1** 1
Information, Asking for **2** 5

Instructions and explanations **1** 1, 8, 13, **2** 2, 6, 11
Introductions **1** 6, **2** 1, 12, 15
Inviting someone out **2** 1
Jobs **1** 8, 15, **2** 8, 14
Lost property office **2** 9
Markets **1** 11
Meeting and introducing **1** 6, **2** 1, 12, 15
Menus **1** 4
Money **1** 10, **2** 5, 6
– currency **1** 3
– prices **1** 4, 11, 14, **2** 7, 13
must/can't (deduction) **2** 13
must/mustn't (obligation) **2** 2
Narrating a series of events **2** 9
Nationalities **1** 3, 4
Numbers **1** 15, **2** 16
Obligation **2** 2
one (*Which one?, the red one*, etc.) **2** 4
Ordering food and drink **1** 1, 4
Parties **2** 1
Passport office **1** 7
Personal details (name, address, family, nationality, job, hobbies, etc.) **1** 6, 7, 9, 10, **2** 4, 9, 14
Persuading **2** 7, 10
Police **1** 13, 15
Postman **2** 4
Post office **1** 9
Present Perfect **2** 10
– with *the first time* **2** 3
Present Perfect Continuous **2** 16
Present Simple/Continuous **1** 2
Prices **1** 4, 11, 14, **2** 7, 13
Psychiatrist **2** 8
Questions and answers **1** 5, 6, 7, **2** 4, 5, 9, 14, 16
Railway station **1** 16
Reception desk (hotel) **1** 14
Rehearsals **2** 15
Renting a car **2** 5
Restaurants **1** 4, **2** 12
Shopping **1** 11
should have + past participle **2** 11
So/Nor (*do I*), etc. **1** 10
so/such **2** 12
Suggestions **1** 16, **2** 8, 10
Superlative adjectives **2** 7
Surprise **1** 6, **2** 3, 12
Telephoning **1** 5, 8, 16, **2** 10
Tickets (train) **1** 2, 16
Tourist information office **2** 5
Tourists **2** 5, 13
Trains **1** 2, 16
Travel agent **2** 10
Travelling,
– by bus **1** 15
– by car **2** 11
– by plane **1** 12
– by train **1** 2, 16
World records **2** 16

1 Gerry Thatcher's party

This sketch was first performed in 1981. Most coursebooks include in their earliest lessons the language used in meeting and greeting people, introducing oneself and others, and so on. A very useful follow-up to this is the language used in inviting someone out, so we included this alongside the former language in this sketch. We chose to set the events at a 'smart' party because of the comic rather than realistic possibilities. The versatile book *English for All Situations* proves just as useful here as it does in Sketch 15, *The bus stop* (in Book 1).

Words and expressions

invitation, *lounge* (= living-room)
actually, *useful*, *wonderful*; *The trouble is…*
pick (someone) up (= call for/collect someone)

In the sketch, the word *Night* leads to confusion: this confusion is possible because *Night* is often used as a contraction of *Good night*. Some British family names have two hyphenated parts: it is this feature which enables the formation of the imaginary name *Smith-Actually*.

Preliminary practice

Put the class into pairs or groups, and ask each pair or group to devise five questions that could be used when inviting someone out. Don't mention the sentences that Horace uses in the sketch (or indeed any specific sentences). Just give some ideas for topics, such as:
- Ask about availability on a particular day.
- Propose an activity.
- Ask if the person likes a particular kind of food, music, films, etc.
- Suggest a means of transport.

When the students have devised their questions, they can try them out on someone from another pair or group, who may answer as they like. The people making the invitations should try to ask all five of their questions, even if they get a negative response early on from the people they are inviting!

Follow-up activities

① As a whole-class activity, the students could improvise a party scene, in which the host introduces several celebrities (famous contemporary or historical figures) to different small groups of other guests – one celebrity to each group. The groups talk to the celebrities about their life, work, interests, and so on. For this activity, the teacher or a student can act as the party host, and periodically move the celebrities around to introduce them to different groups. The host can also periodically interject offers of drinks and snacks.

② Here is another activity connected with the subject of parties, this time involving the students working in groups.

Each group composes an invitation for a party of some kind and writes it on a card or a piece of paper. The text should include the usual information, such as the date, time and place of the party, what it is celebrating, whether the guests should bring something, etc. When these invitations are complete, each group delivers their invitation to another group. Then there are two possible ways to proceed:

a. the groups compose and write a reply to the invitation they have received, and deliver this written reply back to the inviting group;
b. each group nominates one person to 'telephone' a person in the inviting group and reply to the invitation orally.

Props and costumes

For classroom re-enacting, you will need a table, a book (placed on the table until needed), and some empty glasses (plastic ones are more practical than real ones). The doorbell sound can be done vocally.

For a more elaborate performance, you will need the table, made attractive with a tablecloth; plastic glasses; a bottle or two; the book, with the title *English for All Situations* on the cover; a doorbell sound off-stage. Costumes: smart party clothes for Gerry (perhaps a dinner-jacket) and Amanda (perhaps a long dress); a bow-tie and smart shirt for Maxwell; and for Horace something slightly awkward, e.g. a non-matching shirt and tie, and trousers which are a little short.

Gerry Thatcher's party

Scene   A smart party
Characters   Gerry Thatcher, the host
Maxwell, Gerry's butler
Horace Smith ⎤
Amanda Spencer ⎦ guests at the party

The doorbell rings. Maxwell opens the door.

Maxwell	Yes, sir?
Horace	Er…Hello. Is this Gerry Thatcher's house?
Maxwell	Yes, sir.
Horace	Oh, good. I've got an invitation to Gerry's party. My name's Horace Smith.
Maxwell	In that case, please come in, sir.
Horace	Thank you.
Maxwell	Mr Thatcher is in the lounge. This way.
Horace	Er…Thank you.

They go into the lounge, where the party is in progress. Horace sees Gerry.

Horace	Er…Hello.
Gerry	George!
Horace	What?
Gerry	George Wilberforce!
Horace	Pardon?
Gerry	How are you, George?
Horace	Actually, I'm not –
Gerry	Good, good, good!
Horace	No, just a minute –
Gerry	How's your wife?
Horace	I'm not married.
Gerry	Good, good, good!

The doorbell rings again.

Gerry	Maxwell, give George a drink. I'll go to the door.
Maxwell	Yes, sir.

Gerry opens the door.

Amanda   Gerry!

Gerry   Amanda! How are you?

Amanda   Fine.

Gerry   Good, good, good! Come in, come in, come in.

Amanda   Thank you.

Gerry brings Amanda over to Horace.

Gerry   Amanda, I'd like you to meet one of my oldest friends – George Wilberforce.

Amanda   How do you do, George.

Horace   Actually, my name *isn't* George.

Gerry   Isn't it?

Horace   No.

Gerry   What is it, then?

Horace   It's Horace Smith, actually.

Gerry   Of course it is! Amanda, I'd like you to meet one of my *dearest* friends, Horace Smith-Actually.

Horace   It's just *Smith*, actually.

Gerry   That's what I said.

Amanda   I'm very pleased to meet you, Mr Actually.

Horace   No, it's *Smith*, actually.

Amanda   Oh, yes. Mr Smith-Actually.

Horace   No, no, no…My name isn't Smith-Actually, actually. It's just *Smith*, actually.

Gerry   I'm sure it is. Have a drink. Amanda?

Amanda   Yes, Gerry?

Gerry   Come and have a look at the garden.

Amanda   OK.

Amanda goes into the garden with Gerry.

Maxwell   Your drink, sir.

Horace   Thank you. She's very nice, isn't she?

Maxwell   Yes, sir. Very nice indeed.

Horace   I'd like to go out with her.

Maxwell   Would you, sir?

Horace   Yes, very much. The trouble is, I never know what to say when I meet people.

Maxwell   In that case, sir, I think you need this book.

Maxwell shows Horace a book.

Horace   What is it?

Maxwell	'English for all situations', sir. It's full of useful expressions. Look – 'Unit 1: In a restaurant.'…'Unit 2: On a train.'…'Unit 3: At a party. Useful expressions in English, when you meet someone at a party.'
Horace	Wonderful.
Maxwell	(**Reading**) 'Are you doing anything on Saturday night?'
Horace	No, I'm not, actually.
Maxwell	No, sir. That's the first question. Try it.
Horace	Ah. Are you doing anything on Saturday night?
Maxwell	Good. 'How about going to the cinema?'
Horace	How about going to the cinema?
Maxwell	'What time shall I pick you up?'
Horace	Pardon?
Maxwell	That's the next expression.
Horace	Ah. What time shall I pick you up?
Maxwell	I think, sir, that you should suggest doing something before going to the cinema.
Horace	Good idea. What, for example?
Maxwell	Well, going to a restaurant – an Italian restaurant, perhaps.
Horace	OK.
Maxwell	So you say: 'Do you like Italian food?'
Horace	Do you like Italian food?
Maxwell	*She'll* say 'Yes', because everyone likes Italian food. So *you* say. 'So do I.'
Horace	So do I.
Maxwell	'Let's have *spaghetti alle vongole* before we go.'
Horace	Let's have *spaghetti on a gondola* before we go.
Maxwell	Hmm…And finally you say: 'See you on Saturday!'
Horace	See you on Saturday!
Maxwell	Good. Now let's practise.
Horace	Right. Um…Are you doing anything on Saturday morning?
Maxwell	Night.
Horace	Oh, good night.
Maxwell	Saturday *night*, sir. Try again.
Horace	Are you doing anything on Saturday night?
Maxwell	(**In a high voice**) No, I'm not.
Horace	What?…Oh, I see. Er…good. How about going to the cinema?
Maxwell	(**In a high voice**) I'd love to.
Horace	What time…shall I pick you up?
Maxwell	(**In a high voice**) Eight o'clock?
Horace	Do you like Italian food?

Maxwell	(*In a high voice*) Yes, I *love* Italian food.
Horace	So do I. Let's have…*spaghetti alle vongole* before we go.
Maxwell	(*In a high voice*) That would be lovely.
Horace	See you on Saturday!
Maxwell	Very good, sir. Now, take the book, and have a little practice before she comes back.
Horace	Right. Thank you.

Horace concentrates on the book. Gerry and Amanda come back from the garden, laughing.

Amanda	Oh, Gerry, you're awfully funny!
Gerry	Yes, I know. Amanda?
Amanda	Yes, Gerry?
Gerry	Are you doing anything on Saturday night?
Amanda	No, I'm not.
Gerry	Super! How about going to the cinema?
Amanda	Oh, Gerry, that would be wonderful.
Gerry	Super! What time shall I pick you up?
Amanda	Eight o'clock?
Gerry	Super!

The doorbell rings again.

Gerry	It's all right, Maxwell – I'll go. See you on Saturday, Amanda!
Amanda	OK, Gerry.

Gerry goes to open the door. Amanda goes over to Horace.

Amanda	Oh, hello. I don't think we've met.
Horace	Yes, we have, Amanda. It's me – Horace.
Amanda	Horace?
Horace	Yes, Horace Smith.
Amanda	Oh, yes – Mr Actually.

They laugh.

Horace	Er…Amanda?
Amanda	Yes, Horace?

Horace looks at the book.

Horace	(*Reading*) 'Are you doing anything on Saturday night?'
Amanda	Yes, I am.
Horace	(*Still reading*) 'Good. How about going to the cinema?'

Amanda   Actually, I'm going to the cinema with *Gerry* on Saturday night.

Horace   'What time shall I pick you up?'

Amanda   Horace, I'm going out with *Gerry* on Saturday night.

Horace   'Do you like Italian food?'

Amanda   No, I *hate* Italian food.

Horace   'So do I. Let's have *spaghetti on a gondola* before we go.'

Amanda   Oh, Horace, you *are* funny. Why don't we go for a walk in the garden?

Horace   'See you on Saturday!'

Amanda   (***Laughing***) Oh, Horace!

They go into the garden.

2 The army

This sketch was first performed in 1987. The script as given here is the stage version in full, with the exception of a short, mainly visual, section in which the captain demonstrates to the unimpressed privates some 'secret signs' supposedly used by enemy agents, which has been omitted. As noted in connection with Sketch 13, *The police* (in Book 1), we have often found useful comic possibilities in groups of people in uniform who fall short of the dignity and efficiency they aim for.

Words and expressions

Connected with the army:
captain, private, Halt!, Attention!
the enemy, attack (vb.), *enemy agents*

Other expressions:
cap, glasses (= spectacles), *lazy, cross the road, recognize, not necessarily*

Note that *the enemy* is treated as a plural noun: '*If the enemy know* that we get up at five o'clock…*They'll* attack us at four o'clock.'

Preliminary practice

The army is traditionally an environment in which one does what one is told, so some practice of giving and obeying instructions may be a useful preparation for this sketch.

You could use an activity of the type usually associated with the Total Physical Response technique. Such activities usually involve the teacher – and then the students – giving instructions to members of the class, which the members of the class carry out. These instructions can start very simply: for example, *Get up. Walk across the room. Pick up a book*, etc.

Once the idea is established, the class can think of some military-style instructions to be carried out, such as *March!, Left, right! Left, right!, Stand to attention!, Stand at ease!*, for example.

Follow-up activities

① In the sketch, the soldiers discuss things which one *must* do and things which one *mustn't* do in the army. Some of these things are 'reasonable' in the army context (*You must get up at five o'clock in the morning, You must never give information to enemy agents*) and some are not 'reasonable' (*You mustn't cross the road*). The students may like to devise their own version of the sketch, in which they replace these rules with different ones.

② The sketch ends with the soldiers marching off to the pub for lunch, under instructions to all buy the captain a drink. The students could improvise a continuation of the sketch to cover the scene at the pub. This would involve five students – the four characters from the sketch, plus a person serving at the bar. The general shape of the scene could be as follows:

The captain and the privates arrive at the pub, still marching, and march up to the bar.
They order drinks.
One private pays for the drinks, and the others each reimburse a third of the cost.
They then look at a list of sandwiches available at the bar*, and each order something.
They then march over to a table with their drinks and food, and sit down.

*You could provide the list, e.g. **Sandwiches**: *Ham, Cheese, Chicken, Ham and Cheese, Ham and Chicken, Ham Salad, Chicken Salad*, etc.

Props and costumes

This sketch needs no props at all, either for simple classroom re-enacting or for a more elaborate performance (although the captain may like to have a whistle with which to silence the privates on the occasions when he calls *Silence!*, etc.).

Costumes needed for a performance would be, of course, army uniforms as appropriate for the captain and the privates. The captain's hat is a peaked cap, the privates' hats are berets or forage-caps. Potter should either be without a hat, or be wearing a hat which doesn't match those worn by Large and Small.

The army

Scene	A British army base
Characters	A Captain
	Private Large
	Private Small
	Private Potter

The Captain, Private Large and Private Small arrive, marching.

Captain	Left, right! Left, right! Left, right! Halt! Attention!…Private Large!
Large	Sir!
Captain	Private Small!
Small	Sir!
Captain	Private Potter!…Private Potter!…Where is Private Potter?
Large	I don't know, sir!
Small	Haven't seen him, sir!
Captain	Private Potter!!

Potter arrives in not-very-military style.

Potter	Here I am! Hello! Sorry I'm a bit late – I couldn't find my cap.
Captain	Get in line, Private Potter! Left, right! Left, right! Left, right! Attention!

Potter is now in line with Large and Small.

Potter	(**To Large and Small**) Did you take my cap?
Captain	Private Potter!
Potter	Yes?
Captain	Yes, *sir*.
Potter	Captain, you don't have to call me 'sir' – I'm a private.
Captain	Private Potter, when *you* speak to *me*, *you* call *me* 'sir'!
Potter	Oh, sorry – I forgot…sir.
Captain	That's better. Now, I want to talk to you. In fact, I want to talk to *all* of you. You're in the army, right?
Large **Small** **Potter**	Right!
Captain	And in the army, there are some things you *must* do, and some things you *mustn't* do. Isn't that right, Private Large?
Large	Pardon, sir?

Captain   In the army, there are some things you *must* do and some things you *mustn't* do.

Large   Yes, sir!

Captain   Give me an example!

Large   I don't know, sir!

Captain   Private Large?

Large   Yes, sir!

Captain   You're an idiot!

Large   Thank you, sir!

Captain   Private Small!

Small   Yes, sir?

Captain   Give me an example!

Small   An example of what, sir?

Captain   An example of something you *must* do in the army!

Small   Oh right, sir. Er…

Captain   Come on!

Small   You must get up in the morning, sir!

Captain   What?

Small   You must get up in the morning, sir!

Captain   No, Private Small, that's wrong. Correct him, Private Potter.

Potter   You *mustn't* get up in the morning?

Captain   No!…Private Large!

Large   Yes, sir!

Captain   Did you hear Private Small's example?

Large   Yes, sir!

Captain   It was wrong, wasn't it?

Large   Yes, sir!

Captain   Why was it wrong?

Large   I don't know, sir!

Captain   Private Large?

Large   Yes, sir?

Captain   You're still an idiot!

Large   Thank you, sir!

Captain   Listen. Getting up in the morning is not just an army rule. *Everyone* has to get up in the morning.

Potter   Not necessarily, sir. A lot of people don't have to get up in the morning.

Captain   You mean *lazy* people, Private Potter?

Potter   No, not *lazy* people – people who work at nights.

Small   Or in the afternoon.

Large	Or in the evening!
Captain	Silence! All right, all right. The rule in the army is this: You must get up at *five o'clock* in the morning. Isn't that right, Private Large?
Large	Yes, sir!
Captain	Isn't that right, Private Small?
Small	Yes, sir!
Captain	Isn't that right, Private Potter?
Potter	Yes, sir!…But it's stupid.
Captain	What was that?
Potter	It's stupid getting up at five o'clock in the morning.
Captain	Why is it stupid getting up at five o'clock in the morning, Private Potter?
Potter	It's too early.
Captain	Too early?!
Potter	Yes. It's much too early.
Large	I agree, sir!
Small	So do I, sir!
Potter	Why can't we stay in bed until seven o'clock?
Small	Or eight o'clock?
Large	Or lunchtime?
Captain	Silence! You have to get up at five o'clock in the morning because –
Large **Small** **Potter**	Yes?
Captain	Because we may be attacked by the enemy!
Large **Small**	Ah!
Potter	But that's also stupid.
Captain	What?
Potter	If the enemy know that we get up at *five* o'clock –
Large **Small**	Yes?
Potter	They'll attack us at *four* o'clock.
Large **Small**	Oh yes!
Potter	So…if we stay in bed until twelve o'clock midday –
Large **Small**	Yes?
Potter	The enemy will come at *eleven* o'clock!
Large **Small**	Oh yes!

Potter	And that's a much better time to be attacked.
Large	I agree, sir!
Small	So do I, sir!
Potter	And another thing –
Captain	Silence! Private Potter, you are wrong! You must get up at five o'clock!
Potter	But why?
Captain	Because you're in the army. It's an army rule. Now, can anybody tell me something you *mustn't* do in the army?
Small	Yes, sir!
Captain	Well done, Private Small. Let's have your example. What *mustn't* you do in the army?
Small	You mustn't cross the road, sir!
Captain	Eh?
Small	When the little man is red, sir!
Captain	What?
Small	You mustn't cross the road when the little man is red, sir.
Captain	*What* little man, Private Small?
Small	The little man on the crossing, sir. On the red light, sir.
Large	He's right, sir. You must wait until the little man is green, sir.
Captain	Private Large!
Large	Yes, sir?
Captain	You know I said you were an idiot…
Large	Yes, sir?
Captain	I was wrong.
Large	Thank you, sir!
Captain	You and Private Small are *both* idiots!
Large **Small**	} Thank you, sir!
Captain	'You mustn't cross the road when the little man is red.' Do you *really* think that's something you mustn't do in the army?
Small	Yes, sir.
Captain	Private Small, you must understand the difference between *general* rules and *army* rules. There are special rules just for the army.
Large	Can you give us an example, sir?
Captain	Yes, Private Large – an example. You must never give information to enemy agents!
Large **Small** **Potter**	} You must never give information to enemy agents!
Small	Excuse me, sir.
Captain	What is it, Small?

Small	How do you recognize an enemy agent, sir?
Captain	Well, they are either men –
Large **Small** **Potter**	Yes.
Captain	– or women.
Large **Small** **Potter**	Oh.
Captain	Some of them wear dark glasses –
Large **Small** **Potter**	Yes.
Captain	– some of them wear ordinary glasses –
Large **Small** **Potter**	Ooh!
Captain	– and some of them –
Large **Small** **Potter**	Yes?
Captain	– don't wear glasses at all!

Large, Small and Potter panic.

Captain	Silence! Now, what have we learnt about life in the army? Private Large!
Large	You must get up at five o'clock in the morning, sir!
Captain	Correct. Private Small!
Small	You must never give information to enemy agents, sir!
Captain	Correct. Private Potter!
Potter	You must always call the Captain 'sir'…sir.
Captain	Right! It's time for lunch. We can all go down to the pub. And don't forget the most important rule of all.
Potter	What's that?
Captain	You must all buy *me* a drink! Left, right! Left, right! Left, right!…

They all march away.

3 The dentist

The idea for this sketch came from a member of the ETT who had studied to be a dentist. It was first performed in 1975. In the stage version, it is a very visual sketch with a very large number of props, so we have rewritten it somewhat for this book. It has, in fact, been used in ETT shows in several versions over the years, including a 1992 rewrite in which the patients were Batman and Superman, and the dentist had an assistant, with those two characters turning out to be Catwoman and Parrotwoman respectively.

Words and expressions

molar, anaesthetic, extraction, injection, string, hammer (n.), *superstitious, work* (vb.) in *It works!, How does it work?* and *That worked very well.*

Note the rather formal tone of *What seems to be the matter?* and *I'll be with you in a moment.*

The sketch includes several examples of the Present Perfect tense, including its use after expressions such as *It's/This is the first time... .*

Preliminary practice

The sketch begins with a man and a woman 'making conversation' in the waiting-room. The students could improvise some short conversations of this type. Here is a possible way of doing this:

Put the students into groups of three, and give each group a 'waiting' situation (e.g. a doctor's waiting-room, a bus shelter, an airport departure lounge; the groups do not all have to have *different* situations). They begin with one person sitting and waiting. Another person arrives, and the two of them 'make conversation' for a few moments: they can say anything which feels appropriate, and it doesn't have to be complicated! The third person then arrives and joins in the conversation. (The students can simply work in their groups, or they could 'perform' for the rest of the class.)

Follow-up activities

① In the sketch, the man and the woman have to deal with the 'dentist' who is very insistent about what he intends to do. The students could improvise dialogues in similar situations; for example:

Shopkeeper and customer: the customer only wants a box of matches, but the shopkeeper wants to sell something large and expensive.

Patient and doctor: the patient has a headache, but the doctor insists on examining his/her foot.

Celebrity (rock star, film star, Prime Minister) and person in street: the celebrity is busy, but the person insists on taking him/her home for a cup of tea.

Cue-cards would be useful for this activity. For example, the customer's card could read:
You are a customer in a shop. You only want a box of matches. Do not buy anything else.

And the shopkeeper's card could read:
You are a shopkeeper. Try to sell the customer something large and expensive. If the customer says 'No', insist.

② Elicit and write on the board things which, like visiting the dentist, may make people nervous: for example, flying, high places, snakes, horror films, large crowds, etc. The students can then discuss in groups, choosing something which makes them nervous, saying why, and adding any personal anecdotes they have about it.

Props and costumes

For simple classroom re-enacting, if possible put a few magazines on a low table or desk in front of the chairs used by the man and woman: this will suggest a waiting-room, and the characters can flip through them during the opening part of the sketch. A bag of some sort is useful for the 'dentist'.

For a more elaborate performance, you will also need some pieces of string, a hammer, forceps and a syringe (these last three preferably toy ones); and scissors, socks and trousers in the bag used by the 'dentist'. Costumes: as desired for the man and woman; perhaps white jackets for the 'dentist' and the real dentist.

The dentist

Scene A dentist's waiting-room
Characters Two patients: a man and a woman
A 'dentist'
The real dentist

The man and the woman are sitting in the waiting-room. The woman is calm, but the man is very nervous.

Man Um....is he good?

Woman Pardon?

Man The dentist. Is he good?

Woman I don't know.

Man You don't know?

Woman No. I haven't seen him before. He's new.

Man New!?

Woman Yes. It's his first day.

Man Oh…This is *my* first visit, you know.

Woman Oh, really?

Man It's the first time I've been here.

Woman Oh.

Man Don't you understand? It's the first time I've been to the dentist in my life!

Woman I see.

The man looks at his watch.

Man He's late, isn't he?

Woman Well, it *is* his first day.

Man Oh well, perhaps I won't wait. I can come back tomorrow…or the next day.

They hear the dentist coming.

Woman Ah, here he comes now.

Man (*Disappointed*) Oh, good.

The 'dentist' comes in, carrying a large bag.

'Dentist' Ah, good morning, good morning, good morning. Sorry I'm late. Now, who's first?

Woman He was here first.

Man Oh no, after you.

Woman	No, no, you were before me.
Man	No, no, ladies first.
'Dentist'	Now, now, what seems to be the matter?
Man	I've got a bad tooth.
Woman	So have I.
'Dentist'	Well, I can do you both at the same time.
Man **Woman** }	Both at the same time?
'Dentist'	Yes. I've got two pieces of string. Look!
Woman	String? To take out a tooth? Have you done that before?
'Dentist'	Not on people, no. But I tried it this morning on the cat.
Woman	And was the cat all right?
'Dentist'	Oh, yes! It got up, ran across the room, and jumped out of the window. And we live on the thirteenth floor.
Woman	The thirteenth floor?
'Dentist'	Don't worry, the cat's not superstitious.
Man	But dentists don't use *string* to take out teeth!
'Dentist'	Don't they? What do you want, then?
Man	Well, to begin with, I'd like an anaesthetic.
'Dentist'	Oh, you'd like an anaesthetic, would you? Just a minute.

He takes a hammer out of his bag.

'Dentist'	Ah, yes. Here we are.
Woman	What's that?
'Dentist'	A hammer.
Man	Ah! Is that the anaesthetic?
'Dentist'	I'm not sure. It's the first time I've given an anaesthetic. Sit still.

He hits the table; this frightens the man, who faints.

Man	Oh! Ohh!
'Dentist'	Oh, it works!

He puts the hammer down.

'Dentist'	Now, madam, what's the matter with you?
Woman	I've got a pain.
'Dentist'	Where?
Woman	In my mouth.
'Dentist'	Yes, I know it's in your mouth, but which tooth?
Woman	This one here.

'Dentist'	Ah yes, a molar.
Woman	What are you going to do?
'Dentist'	I'm going to take it out.
Woman	How?
'Dentist'	I don't know.
Woman	You don't know?
'Dentist'	No. This is the first time I've taken out a molar. In fact, it's the first time I've taken out a tooth.
Woman	The first time you've taken out a tooth!
'Dentist'	Yes. This is a very important day for me – my first extraction. Now, where's that hammer?
Woman	Listen, I don't want the hammer and I don't want the string. I want you to take my tooth out with a pair of –
'Dentist'	A pair of scissors?
Woman	No.
'Dentist'	A pair of socks?
Woman	No.
'Dentist'	A pair of trousers?
Woman	No.
'Dentist'	Oh. Just a minute.

He looks inside his bag, and takes out a large pair of forceps.

'Dentist'	These?
Woman	Yes, I suppose so.
'Dentist'	Right then. Open your mouth.
Woman	But what about the anaesthetic?
'Dentist'	Oh yes. Pass me the hammer.
Woman	I don't *want* the hammer! I want a *proper* anaesthetic. I want an injection.
'Dentist'	An injection?
Woman	Yes.
'Dentist'	Just a minute.

He looks inside his bag again, and takes out a large syringe.

'Dentist'	Ah yes, this is for injections, isn't it? How does it work?
Woman	Well, you're the dentist. Don't *you* know?
'Dentist'	No. It's the first time I've used one of these. Oh well, I'll have a try. Open your mouth.
Woman	Er, no…I don't think you really know…er…no, no, I'll come back another day. I –

The man wakes up.

Man	Where am I? Hey, what are you doing?

'Dentist'   I'll be with you in a moment, sir. Now, just sit still, madam…

Man   No, no, stop that! You're absolutely crazy!

Woman   I agree. He's absolutely crazy, completely mad. Let's get out of here.

Man   Oh yes, good idea.

'Dentist'   So you don't want me to take out that molar?

Woman   Certainly not. (**To the man**) Come on.

Man   Yes. Good idea.

The man and the woman leave.

'Dentist'   Hmm, that worked very well.

He puts his things into the bag, laughing to himself.

'Dentist'   'But dentists don't use *string* to take out teeth!' – 'Oh, you'd like an anaesthetic, would you?'

The real dentist arrives.

Dentist   Oh, good morning. Sorry I'm late. It's my first day. It's the first time I've been here. Are you the only one?

'Dentist'   Yes, there's just me.

Dentist   Right. You can come straight in, then.

'Dentist'   Oh, good. I hate having to wait.

© Macmillan Publishers Limited 1995.

Mr Williams and the postman 4

The idea for this sketch came from a classroom activity: a revision activity with a class of intermediate students, whose common mistake was to omit the word *one* in expressions such as *the red one* or *the Japanese one*. The sketch itself was first performed in 1976. In the original stage version, the ending was slightly different: Mrs Williams won a weekend in Brighton with the postman; this ending has subsequently been modified and it is a modified version which is used in the script given here.

Words and expressions

envelope, competition, star prize, win,
unhappy, unfortunate, exciting, ridiculous, silly,
What's going on? (= What's happening?), *Concentrate!,*
Stop wasting our time.

The expression *the Post Office*, as used in the sketch, means the organization responsible for postal services, not one particular post office in the street. Note the use of stress for contrast (e.g. 'I want the *blue* one') and for emphasis ('Today's *star prize*…').

Preliminary practice

Here is an activity focusing on expressions such as *the red one*, *the blue one*, etc.: Put the students into groups and give each group several pieces of card, of varied colours. On some cards, the students draw pictures of objects (one picture per card) and on others they write the words corresponding to the objects (one word per card).*

In random order and with the plain side visible, stick the cards in lines on the board, or place them on a table, ensuring that all the cards in any given line are of different colours. The students have to try to find the matching pictures and words by asking to see two cards, e.g. *Can I see the red one in the top line and the green one in the second line?* The activity continues until all the matching pairs have been revealed.

*Note: the activity works best if there are at least 16 cards in total, and if no picture is on the same colour card as its corresponding word.

Follow-up activities

① The students could improvise the dialogue that would have taken place if Mr and Mrs Williams had opened the white envelope and found the cheque for £500: firstly the dialogue with the postman, and secondly the dialogue between themselves (after the postman has gone), speculating on what they will do with the money.

② The students could act out a TV quiz game in which prizes can be won. In groups, they make up the questions – six questions per group, for example – and decide on the prizes. The questions could be either about general knowledge or questions about English words, places or institutions (similar to the postman's first two questions in the sketch). One group can then appoint a 'presenter', who will put the group's questions to 'contestants' from another group. All the groups take a turn in this way. In playing the game, the presenters could use expressions like these:

Here's the first question.
The prize is (a bottle of milk)!
Congratulations! You've won the (bottle of milk)!
Listen carefully.
Never mind – try another question.
Today's star prize is (a holiday in Scotland).

Some suspense could be added by making the game one of the 'all-or-nothing' variety, i.e. if a team wins five prizes, but fails to answer the sixth question correctly, they lose all their prizes.

Props and costumes

For simple classroom re-enacting, all that is needed is three envelopes – appropriately coloured, if possible – two with pieces of paper inside (representing the note and the cheque) and one empty.

For a more elaborate performance, you will need the coloured envelopes, the note, the cheque, and a bag for the postman. Costumes: a uniform for the postman, and perhaps dressing-gowns, slippers, etc. for Mr and Mrs Williams. There is no need for an actual door: opening and closing it can be mimed, and the sounds of knocking and ringing the bell can be made by the postman.

Mr Williams and the postman

Scene The front door of 65 Shakespeare Avenue, early one morning
Characters A postman
Mr Henry Williams
Mrs Agnes Williams

The postman walks up to the front door. He knocks at the door and rings the bell.

Postman Good morning! Hello! Wake up!

Mr Williams opens the door.

Postman Ah, good morning!

Henry Good morning.

Postman Mr Williams?

Henry Yes.

Postman Mr *H.* Williams?

Henry That's right.

Postman Mr *Henry* Williams of 65 Shakespeare Avenue?

Henry Sixty-five? Er…yes. Have you got anything for me?

Postman No.

Henry No?

Postman No.

Henry Then why did you wake me up?

Postman It's part of my job.

Henry What? Waking people up?

Postman Yes. It's a new service from the Post Office.

Henry Hmm. Listen – you're a postman.

Postman Yes.

Henry And postmen bring letters.

Postman Yes.

Henry But you haven't brought any for me.

Postman Wait a minute, Mr Williams. I'm sure I can find something for you. Um…

He takes three letters out of his bag.

Postman Ah yes, here we are. Three letters. Which one would you like? The red one, the white one, or the blue one?

Henry	But those letters aren't for me.
Postman	No, Mr Williams, but this is another new service from the Post Office – a new service for all those unhappy, unfortunate people who never get any letters.
Henry	Oh.
Postman	And you, Mr Williams, you never get any letters, do you?
Henry	No, I don't.
Postman	All right then, which one would you like? The red one, the white one, or the blue one?
Henry	Um…I'll have the red one, please.
Postman	The red one is yours – if you can answer a simple question.
Henry	A question?
Postman	Yes. Where does Queen Elizabeth the Second of England live?
Henry	Why? Have you got a letter for her?

He laughs.

Postman	No, Mr Williams. That was the question. Where does Queen Elizabeth the Second of England live?
Henry	Ah. Where does Queen Elizabeth live?
Postman	Yes.
Henry	I don't know.
Postman	Mr Williams! It's easy! B-B-B-Buck –
Henry	Oh, yes! Buckingham Hotel.
Postman	No, no! Palace!
Henry	Palace Hotel.
Postman	No!
Henry	I know! Buckingham Palace!
Postman	That's right! You've won the red envelope!
Henry	Oh, thank you! This is very exciting!

Mr Williams opens the red envelope.

Henry	There's nothing in it.
Postman	No, there's never anything in the red one.
Henry	This is ridiculous!
Postman	No, it isn't. There are still two more envelopes.
Henry	Yes, but is there anything in them?
Postman	Of course there is.
Henry	All right. The blue one.
Postman	Very well, Mr Williams. Here is the question for the blue envelope. What is the approximate population of Great Britain?

Henry	Er…thirty-five million?
Postman	No. Higher.
Henry	Eighty-five million?
Postman	No. Lower.
Henry	Fifty-five million people!
Postman	– is the correct answer! You've won the white envelope!
Henry	I don't *want* the white one. I want the *blue* one.
Postman	Oh, go on. Take the white one.
Henry	I don't *want* the white one!
Postman	Oh, all right. Here's the blue one.
Henry	Thank you.

Mr Williams opens the blue envelope.

Henry	Hmm. Just a piece of paper.
Postman	What does it say?
Henry	It says: 'You should have taken the white one.'
Postman	I told you.
Henry	This is very silly. I'm going back to bed.
Postman	Wait a minute, Mr Williams. Today's *star prize* is in the white envelope.
Henry	The star prize?
Postman	Yes.
Henry	All right then, ask me the question.
Postman	Now listen carefully. If a man walks at five miles an hour, in the same direction as a car which is travelling at thirty miles an hour, how long will it take for the car to be 107 miles from the man?
Henry	Eh?
Postman	Mr Williams! Concentrate! If a man walks at five miles an hour, in the same direction as a car which is travelling at thirty miles an hour, how long will it take for the car to be 107 miles from the man?
Henry	I don't know. Three days?
Postman	No, no, Mr Williams. Look, why don't you ask your wife to help you?
Henry	All right. Agnes!
Agnes	Yes?
Henry	Come here!
Agnes	All right. I'm coming.

Mrs Williams comes to the door.

Postman	Ah, good morning, Mrs Williams.
Agnes	What's going on?

© Macmillan Publishers Limited 1995.

Henry	I'm trying to win the white one, Agnes.
Agnes	The white what?
Henry	The white envelope. I've already won the red one and the blue one.
Agnes	Henry, what *are* you talking about?
Henry	It's a competition. We answer questions and win prizes – and the star prize is in the white envelope.
Postman	And here is the question for the white envelope. If a man walks at five miles an hour, in the same direction as a car which is travelling at thirty miles an hour, how long will it take for the car to be 107 miles from the man?
Agnes	That's easy. Four hours, sixteen minutes and forty-eight seconds.
Postman	Four hours, sixteen minutes and forty-eight seconds is the correct answer! You have won today's star prize. Here you are.
Agnes	Ooh, thank you!
Henry	Well done, Agnes.

Mrs Williams opens the white envelope.

Henry	What is it?
Agnes	It's just a piece of paper.
Postman	No, it isn't.
Henry	Yes, it is. Look! Just another piece of paper!

They give the postman back the envelope and paper.

Postman	But, Mr Williams…Mrs Williams…
Henry	Stop wasting our time. Come on, Agnes, let's go back to bed.
Postman	But come back! I can explain!

Mr and Mrs Williams go back into the house.

Postman	I'm sure it's not just another piece of paper. There's always a prize in the white one. Let's have a look…It's a cheque…for £500! Mr Williams! Mrs Williams!
Henry	Go away!
Postman	But Mr Williams, you've won the star prize!
Henry	Go away!!
Postman	Oh…Well, if Mr Williams doesn't want the £500, I think I'll keep it…It's a lovely day today…

He walks away, singing to himself.

5 Tourist information

This sketch was first performed in 1992, although it developed from an earlier sketch set at a tourist information desk which we originally performed in 1985. In the stage version, the sketch takes place on an invented British national holiday called National Banana Day, on which bananas, rather than sterling, are used as currency: this notion is presented prior to the sketch, in a link in which the punch-line for the sketch ('After all, it *is* National Banana Day.') is also given. These rather fanciful ancillary notions are omitted from the script given here.

Words and expressions

Pleased to meet you, What a coincidence!, Congratulations, Enjoy your stay in England, cost (vb.), *owe, rent a car, car rental company, keys* (= car keys), *What is going on here?* (= What is happening here?), *Sydney* (name of city and name of person)

The colloquial expression *come on* (in *No, come on – this is a joke, isn't it?*) means 'stop being unreasonable', 'be serious'.

Preliminary practice

As preparation for this sketch, it may be useful to practise the kind of questions which tourists ask when they arrive – or before they arrive – in the country they are visiting.

Put the students into pairs and ask each pair to devise a short dialogue between a tourist and a tourist information officer in a particular country. The pairs then act out their dialogues for the rest of the class, who guess which country is being enquired about. For example, if the dialogue includes this exchange:

Student A: *I like skiing very much. Are there any mountains here?*
Student B: *No, not really – the country is very flat.*

the rest of the class may ask if the country being enquired about is the Netherlands.

Follow-up activities

① Near the end of the sketch, the tourist realizes that it is possible to request information without using direct questions. He says: *I'd like to rent a car... And I'd like you to tell me where I can do it*, not *Where can I rent a car?* Here is an activity based on that idea:

Put the students into groups. In their groups, they think of three pieces of information they would like to know about a particular country. (These could be the types of information from the preliminary practice.) They must then think of ways of getting this information without asking direct questions – a different way for each of the three pieces of information they want to obtain. For example:
We'd like to know *if there are any mountains.*
We'd like you to tell us *what the climate is like.*
We need to find out *the name of the capital city.*
When the groups have prepared their sentences, each group then tells the class the country they are enquiring about and reads their sentences aloud. The other groups give the information if they can.

② The students could improvise some short dialogues at a car rental company – in twos (clerk and customer) or in threes (clerk and pair of customers). The customers should say the type of car they want, how long they want it for, and can add special requests (e.g. the car must be green or have a radio) making their requests as unusual as they like.

Props and costumes

For classroom re-enacting, you will need a table or desk to represent the information desk, a horn (or something similar to make the noise), and some small cards marked £5, £10, £15, etc. Some pieces of paper to represent the tourist's money, and a set of keys, are also useful.

For a performance, the table or lectern used for the information desk should have a sign on it reading 'Rita's Tourist Information Office', which can be removed to reveal 'Rita's Rent-A-Car'. The cards marked £5, £10, £15, etc. can be in a container fixed to the desk, so that they can be removed one by one at the appropriate moments (i.e. the card marked £5 is at the front). It is also helpful if the horn is fixed to the desk, thus making it easier for Rita to operate. Also needed: money and keys, as noted above. Costumes: probably a smart uniform for Rita, and holiday clothes for the tourist.

Tourist information

Scene A tourist information office at an international airport in England
Characters Rita, the tourist information officer
An Australian tourist

Rita is behind her desk, on which there is a sign saying 'Rita's Tourist Information Office'. The tourist arrives.

Tourist	G'day!
Rita	Pardon?
Tourist	G'day!
Rita	Sorry, sir, I only speak English.
Tourist	I *am* speaking English. '*Good day!*' It's Australian. It's Australian for 'Hello'.
Rita	Is it?
Tourist	Yes.
Rita	Oh, I see. 'G'day!'
Tourist	(**Holding out his hand**) Wallaby.
Rita	Pardon?
Tourist	Wallaby.
Rita	Ah! (**Shaking his hand**) 'Wallaby'.
Tourist	No, no, no. Wallaby is my *name*.
Rita	Oh, I see. Pleased to meet you, Mr Wallaby.
Tourist	I've come from Sydney.
Rita	Sydney?
Tourist	Yes.
Rita	Sydney who?
Tourist	What?
Rita	Sydney Watt? Who's Sydney Watt?
Tourist	No, no – Sydney is in Australia.
Rita	Sydney's in Australia.
Tourist	Yes.
Rita	Oh, I see. So he couldn't come to England.
Tourist	What?
Rita	*You've* come, but *Sydney* hasn't.
Tourist	No, no, no, no! Sydney is the place where I live.
Rita	Oh, I see.

Tourist	At last!
Rita	Sydney is the name of your *house*.
Tourist	(**Giving up**) Yes, all right.
Rita	So which *town* do you come from?
Tourist	Sydney!!
Rita	So Sydney is the name of your house *and* the name of your town! What a coincidence! So how can I help you?
Tourist	I'd like some information.
Rita	Some information?
Tourist	Yes, some tourist information.
Rita	OK, sir. Welcome to Rita's Tourist Information Office. I can answer all your questions.
Tourist	Good.
Rita	But it will cost you five pounds.
Tourist	Pardon me?

Rita toots a horn and reveals a sign saying '£5'.

Rita	Five pounds. Ask me anything you like: the questions are five pounds each.
Tourist	Five pounds each?
Rita	Was that a question?
Tourist	Yes.

Rita toots the horn again and changes the sign to '£10'.

Rita	That's ten pounds.
Tourist	Just a minute! Do I have to pay you five pounds for every question?

Rita toots the horn again and changes the sign to '£15'.

Rita	Pardon?
Tourist	I said: Do I have to pay you five pounds for every question?

Rita toots the horn again and changes the sign to '£20'.

Rita	Yes, sir.
Tourist	But is this normal?

Rita toots the horn again and changes the sign to '£25'.

Rita	Oh yes, sir. It's quite normal.
Tourist	Is it?

Rita toots the horn again and changes the sign to '£30'.

Rita	Yes, sir.
Tourist	No, come on – this is a joke, isn't it?

They both laugh. Then Rita toots the horn again and changes the sign to '£35'.

Rita	No, sir.
Tourist	Look – all I want is some information.
Rita	What did you say?

Rita toots the horn again and changes the sign to '£40'.

Tourist	I said – Wait a minute! I didn't ask a question then.
Rita	Didn't you?

Rita toots the horn again and changes the sign to '£45'.

Tourist	Look! *You've* just asked two questions and *I'm* paying for them.
Rita	OK, I'm sorry, sir. You can have two *free* questions.
Tourist	Can I?
Rita	That's one.
Tourist	Er…now, what do I want to know?
Rita	And that's two.
Tourist	Look, what is going on here?!

Rita toots the horn again and changes the sign to '£50'.

Rita	Fifty pounds! Congratulations, sir. You now owe me fifty pounds. Now, you can pay me the fifty pounds…*or*…you can answer one simple question and double the fifty pounds to one hundred pounds!
Tourist	(**Confused**) Er…
Rita	Here's the question: How old are you?
Tourist	Twenty-six.

Rita toots the horn.

Rita	– is the correct answer!

She changes the sign to '£100'.

Rita	You now owe me one hundred pounds!

The tourist gives her £100.

Tourist	There you are.
Rita	Thank you, sir.

Rita removes the £100 sign.

Rita	Enjoy your stay in England.
Tourist	Thank you.

The tourist starts to leave but then comes back.

Tourist	Wait a minute – I haven't had any information yet!
Rita	Don't worry, sir. Ask me anything you like – but don't forget: it costs…
Rita Tourist	} …five pounds a question.
Tourist	Right. Five pounds a question. Er…Can you tell me –

Rita is going to toot the horn.

Tourist	– no, no, no, no…Do you know –

Rita is again going to toot the horn.

Tourist	– no, no, no, no, no…Ah. Five pounds a *question*. Right. I'd *like* to *rent* a *car*.
Rita	You'd like to rent a car?
Tourist	Yes. And I'd like *you* to tell *me* where I can *do* it.
Rita	You'd like to rent a car?
Tourist	Yes.
Rita	Well, sir, there is a car rental company in the airport.
Tourist	Good. (**Looking around**) And it's –
Rita	– right here!

Rita changes the 'Tourist Information Office' sign to a 'Rent-a-Car' sign.

Rita	Welcome to Rita's Rent-a-Car.
Tourist	Oh.
Rita	We have cars from all over the world. And I have here, in my hand, the keys to a Rolls-Royce.
Tourist	A Rolls-Royce! Yes, please!
Rita	(**Giving him the keys**) Here you are. That's fifty pounds.
Tourist	(**Giving her the money**) Here you are. Fifty pounds for a Rolls-Royce!
Rita	No, sir. It's fifty pounds for the keys.
Tourist	Oh.
Rita	Now, sir – do you have any more questions?
Tourist	Well, I've only got five pounds left.
Rita	So you can have one more question. What would you like to know?
Tourist	What time is the next plane back to Australia?

Rita toots the horn.

Rita	I don't know, sir.

Rita takes his £5 note.

Rita	Thank you very much. Goodbye.

© Macmillan Publishers Limited 1995.

The bank

The idea for this sketch came from an old joke about writing a cheque to cover an overdraft. We also liked the idea of a customer pretending not to understand a bank manager, and a bank robber who was not very competent, so we combined these elements and wrote this sketch. It was first performed in 1976. For this book, the stage version has been slightly shortened and the ending altered; on stage, Mr Moore and the robber went off together to rob another bank, leaving the manager to sing a song.

Words and expressions

Connected with money in general:
earn, make (= earn), *spend, save, rob, steal*

Connected with banking in particular:
cheque, cheque-book, account, open (an account), in the red, overdrawn

Note that the bank manager uses quite formal language most of the time: for example, *Do sit down, I don't think you quite understand, Just excuse me one moment, I'll get the necessary papers.*

Preliminary practice

You could start by brainstorming words concerning money and banks; this will probably generate some of those listed above. You could also use magazine advertisements for banks as a source of vocabulary; these often suggest that one's local bank is a friendly place with smiling people waiting to help you, and would set the scene for the sketch quite well.

Then ask the students to each think of a reason to give their bank manager in order to justify their being £200 overdrawn: for example, they absolutely had to buy something or to give the money to someone; these reasons can be as fanciful as they like. Even if your students are too young to have experience of meeting a bank manager, they should be able to imagine the situation fairly easily.

Follow-up activities

① The bank manager in the sketch tries to convey to Mr Moore the meaning of the expression *in the red* by paraphrasing it, first giving another word (*overdrawn*) and then giving a full explanation. The students could improvise some dialogues in other situations which involve paraphrasing, such as these:

Traveller and immigration official: The traveller's passport has *expired*.

Customer and shopkeeper: The customer pays with a £10 note which is a *forgery*.

Cue-cards will be useful for this activity. For example, the traveller's card could read:
You are a traveller. Your passport has expired. Pretend you do not understand when the official explains this to you.

And the official's card could read:
You are an immigration official. You are talking to a traveller whose passport has expired. Explain this to the traveller.

② The robber gives Mr Moore a set of instructions for robbing a bank. The students could practise giving some other sets of instructions, such as a recipe or how to make a call from a public telephone. They could work in groups to produce their set of instructions in writing, and the groups could then exchange what they have written with other groups, who decide if the instructions are clear and complete.

Props and costumes

For re-enacting in the classroom, you will need a chair for the manager and a desk for her to sit behind; two other chairs, one for Mr Moore and one for the robber; a cheque-book (or a small notebook to represent it); a bag and a piece of paper for the robber.

For a more elaborate performance, the following extra props are useful: a telephone, nameplate and some papers on the manager's desk; a gun and some bundles of money for the robber. Costumes can be as desired: probably something quite smart for the manager; perhaps a striped sweater for the robber.

The bank

Scene	The manager's office in a bank
Characters	Miss D. Posit, the bank manager
	Monica, Miss Posit's secretary
	Mr Moore, a customer
	A bank robber

Miss Posit is sitting at her desk. The intercom buzzes.

Miss Posit   Yes, Monica?

Monica   Miss Posit, there's a gentlemen to see you. Mr Moore.

Miss Posit   Ah, yes. Mr Moore. Bring him in please, Monica.

Monica   Yes, Miss Posit.

Monica brings Mr Moore in.

Monica   Mr Moore.

Miss Posit   Good morning, Mr Moore.

Mr Moore   Good morning.

Miss Posit   Thank you, Monica.

Monica leaves the office.

Miss Posit   Do sit down, Mr Moore.

Mr Moore   Thank you.

He sits down.

Miss Posit   Now, Mr Moore, the situation is like this. Your account is in the red.

Mr Moore   Pardon?

Miss Posit   In the red.

Mr Moore   I'm sorry. I don't understand.

Miss Posit   In the red. Overdrawn.

Mr Moore   'Overdrawn.' No, I'm sorry. I've never heard that word before in my life.

Miss Posit   It's very simple, Mr Moore. It means that you've taken more money *out* of the bank than you've put *in*.

Mr Moore   Oh, I see. Thank you very much.

Miss Posit   I don't think you quite understand, Mr Moore. It means that you've put in *less* than you've taken out.

Mr Moore   Oh.

Miss Posit   Your account is overdrawn. £200 overdrawn.

Mr Moore	£200 overdrawn. I see. Well, don't worry. I can put that right immediately.
Miss Posit	Oh, good.
Mr Moore	Yes, I'll write you a cheque, shall I?

He takes out his cheque-book and begins to write.

Mr Moore	Now…two hundred pounds…
Miss Posit	Mr Moore, Mr Moore, if you write me a cheque for £200, you'll be overdrawn *more*, Mr Moore.
Mr Moore	I beg your pardon?
Miss Posit	*More*, Mr Moore. M-O-R-E, *more*.
Mr Moore	No, no…*double*-O…M-double-O-R-E, Mr *Moore*. It *is* my name.
Miss Posit	Mr Moore, I don't think you quite understand the situation. You see –

The robber comes in suddenly.

Robber	Nobody move!
Miss Posit	– you see, if you write me a cheque for £200 –
Robber	I said: 'Nobody move!'
Miss Posit	Can I help you?
Robber	That's better. *You* –
Mr Moore	Me?
Robber	Yes. Read this.

He gives Mr Moore a note.

Mr Moore	Oh. OK. Er…(**Reading**) 'Two pounds of tomatoes, six eggs, and a packet of chocolate biscuits.'
Robber	No, no, no. The other side.
Mr Moore	Oh, sorry. Er…(**Reading**) 'Give me all your…honey, or I'll…kiss you.'
Robber	Not *honey* – *money*.
Mr Moore	Oh, sorry. (**Reading**) 'Give me all your *money*, or I'll kiss you.'
Robber	Not *kiss* – *kill!*
Mr Moore	Oh. Er…Miss Posit, I think this is for you.

He gives the note to Miss Posit.

Miss Posit	(**Reading**) 'Give me all your money, or I'll kill you.' I see. Would you sit down for a moment?
Robber	Sit down?
Miss Posit	Yes, I'm very busy at the moment. Please sit over there.
Robber	But –
Miss Posit	I'll be with you in a moment.

The robber sits down.

Miss Posit	Now, Mr Moore. How much do you earn?
Mr Moore	£35 a week.
Robber	Excuse me –
Miss Posit	Just one moment, *please*!...So you earn £35 a week. How much do you spend?
Mr Moore	£70 a week.
Robber	Excuse me -
Miss Posit	One moment, *please*!!...£70 a week. So you spend twice as much as you earn.
Mr Moore	Yes, I earn half as much as I spend.
Miss Posit	How do you do it?
Mr Moore	It's easy. I use my cheque-book.
Miss Posit	Exactly, Mr Moore!
Robber	*Excuse me!*
Miss Posit	Yes!!
Robber	*I* make £2,000 a week.
Miss Posit	£2,000 a week? And how much do you spend?
Robber	£1,000 a week.
Miss Posit	Really? So you *save* £1,000 a week.
Robber	Yes.
Miss Posit	(**Very politely**) Would you like to sit here?
Robber	Thank you.
Miss Posit	Mr Moore, would you sit over there for a moment?

The robber and Mr Moore change places.

Miss Posit	So you save £1,000 a week.
Robber	Yes.
Miss Posit	Tell me...where do you keep this money?
Robber	Here. In this bag.

He puts a large bag full of money on the desk.

Miss Posit	Oh. Oh, yes. Very nice. Um...would you like to open an account, Mr...?
Robber	Mr Steele.
Miss Posit	Steele. I see. S-T-double-E-L-E?
Robber	Yes, that's right.
Miss Posit	Well, just excuse me one moment, Mr Steele, and I'll get the necessary papers.
Robber	Certainly.

Miss Posit leaves the office.

Mr Moore	Excuse me…
Robber	Yes?
Mr Moore	You make £2,000 a week.
Robber	Yes.
Mr Moore	How do you do it?
Robber	I rob banks.
Mr Moore	Oh, I see. You rob banks and *steal* the money.
Robber	Yes.
Mr Moore	How do you do it?
Robber	It's easy. You take a gun –
Mr Moore	I haven't got a gun.
Robber	Oh…well, borrow mine.
Mr Moore	Thank you very much.

Mr Moore takes the gun and fires it.

Robber	Be careful!…You take a gun and you take a note.
Mr Moore	Oh, yes, the note. That's very good. I like that. (**Reading**) 'Two pounds of tomatoes, six eggs –'
Robber	The other side!
Mr Moore	Oh, yes. (**Reading**) 'Give me all your honey, or I'll kiss you!'
Robber	*'Money'* and *'kill'*!
Mr Moore	Oh, yes.
Robber	You take the note, go into the bank, and put the note on the bank manager's desk.
Mr Moore	Is that all?
Robber	Yes.
Mr Moore	I see.

Miss Posit comes back into the office.

Miss Posit	Ah, yes. Now, Mr Steele –
Mr Moore	Give me all your honey…*money*, or I'll kiss…*kill* you.
Miss Posit	Money, Mr Moore? Certainly. Take this bag.

She gives Mr Moore the robber's bag.

Mr Moore	Oh, thank you. That was easy.
Robber	Yes, but –
Miss Posit	Mr Moore, your account is still £200 overdrawn.
Mr Moore	Oh, yes. Well…um…Here you are.

He gives her £200 from the robber's bag.

Mr Moore	£50…£100…£150…£200.
Robber	But…But…
Miss Posit	Thank you, Mr Moore.
Mr Moore	Goodbye.

Mr Moore leaves.

Miss Posit	Now, Mr Steele – your account.
Robber	But…But…But…
Miss Posit	Mr Steele…
Robber	Just a minute! I think something's gone wrong. Hey, you! Come back! Bring back my money – and my gun! Come back!

He runs after Mr Moore.

Miss Posit	(**On the intercom**) Monica, would you bring me some coffee, please? Some *strong black* coffee…

This sketch was first performed in 1974, prompted by the idea that praising the qualities of something when selling it is a useful context in which to demonstrate the use of superlative adjectives. Since the word *superlative* can itself be used to indicate high praise, it seemed an appropriate brand name for the vacuum cleaner being sold. The script given here is almost exactly the same as the stage version. We have used the context of 'selling' in several other sketches, such as Sketch 11 *The shoe stall* (in Book 1), and Sketch 10 *The travel agency* (in this book).

Words and expressions

dust (n.), *carpet, handbag, salesman/woman, sales technique, on the market, smart, economical, effective, revolutionary, boring, colourful, detest, go on* (= continue)

The expression *My goodness me!*, used to express surprise, is rather old-fashioned in tone. Notice the use of *just*, meaning 'only' or 'simply' in *Just £65 to you, madam* and *I'll just go and get some money.*

Preliminary practice

As this sketch involves praising the qualities of something when selling it, a good introduction would be an activity based on some advertisements from newspapers and magazines.

Show the class some advertisements and ask them to tell you what the 'selling point (or points)' – i.e. the main qualities being praised – are in each case. If possible, choose advertisements which include expressions such as *the fastest, the most comfortable, the most economical*, etc., as this will provide some useful practice of superlative adjectives.

Then you can lead into the sketch by telling the students that its title is *The Superlative vacuum cleaner*, and asking them to predict which superlative adjectives they think they will hear.

Follow-up activities

① You could organize some role-playing activities in which the characters change roles as the salesman and the housewife do in the sketch. For example: A police officer stops a motorist for speeding. The police officer is not very competent, so the motorist offers to ask the questions. The dialogue might start with lines similar to those in the sketch, like this:

Police officer: You were driving too fast.
Motorist: That's right.
Police officer: Ah.
Motorist: Well, go on, then.
Police officer: I've finished.
Motorist: Finished? You haven't said very much. What sort of a police officer are you?
Police officer: Not a very good one, I'm afraid.
Motorist: I can see that. Look, *you* get into the car, and *I'll* ask the questions.

Some other possible situations: shop assistant and customer; manager explaining job to new employee; geography teacher and student who knows more about geography than the teacher; journalist and politician.

② The students, individually or in groups, could design an advertisement for the 'Superlative' vacuum cleaner, using information from the sketch, inventing a slogan, and adding a drawing and other details such as where it can be bought.

Props and costumes

For simple classroom re-enacting, any object can be used to represent the vacuum cleaner (for example, a wastepaper basket, a pile of books, a bag). Some pieces of paper can be used to represent the money.

For a more elaborate performance, a real vacuum cleaner is needed, and costumes for the characters as desired. As always, it is fun – and more practical – for the door to be mimed and for the doorbell sound to be made vocally by the characters.

The Superlative vacuum cleaner

Scene The hall of a house
Characters A vacuum cleaner salesman
A housewife

The salesman rings the doorbell several times.

Housewife Yes, I'm coming.

She opens the door.

Housewife Good morning.

Salesman Good morning, young lady. Is your mother in?

Housewife My mother? I'm the mother in this house. What do you want?

Salesman Dust, madam.

Housewife Dust?

Salesman Yes, madam. Dust.

Housewife I haven't got any dust.

Salesman Oh yes you have!

He shakes dust onto the floor from a paper bag.

Salesman All over your carpet!

Housewife Hey! I've just cleaned this carpet! Why are you putting dust all over it?

Salesman Don't worry, madam. I've got the answer to all your problems *here*! The Superlative vacuum cleaner!

Housewife The Superlative vacuum cleaner! Why's it called 'Superlative'?

Salesman Because, madam, everything about it *is* superlative. It's the quickest, the cleanest, the cheapest, the smallest, the smartest, the most economical, the most effective, the most beautiful, the most revolutionary vacuum cleaner in the world. And it's only £65.

Housewife Are you trying to sell me a vacuum cleaner?

Salesman Yes, madam.

Housewife Well, go on, then.

Salesman I've finished, madam.

Housewife Finished? You haven't said very much. What sort of a vacuum cleaner salesman are you?

Salesman Not a very good one, I'm afraid.

Housewife I can see that.

Salesman No, I'm a very *bad* vacuum cleaner salesman. In fact, I'm the worst salesman in our company.

Housewife   The worst?

Salesman   The worst. I sometimes think I'm the worst vacuum cleaner salesman in the world.

Housewife   Oh, dear. Do you…like your job?

Salesman   Like my job? No, madam. I detest my job. It's the most boring job in the world. Every day it's the same: 'Good morning, young lady. Is your mother in?…The Superlative vacuum cleaner…The quickest, the cleanest, the cheapest, the smallest…'

Housewife   Well, *is* it the quickest?

Salesman   No, it's probably the slowest.

Housewife   Is it the cleanest?

Salesman   Cleanest? Don't make me laugh! I don't think there's a dirtier vacuum cleaner on the market. And it certainly isn't the cheapest either.

Housewife   No, no, no. This is no good at all.

Salesman   Pardon?

Housewife   Look, do you want to sell this vacuum cleaner or don't you?

Salesman   I suppose so.

Housewife   Well, your sales technique is all wrong.

Salesman   Is it?

Housewife   Yes. I could sell vacuum cleaners better than you.

Salesman   No, you couldn't.

Housewife   Yes, I could. I'll show you. You come into the house, and I'll ring the bell and sell the vacuum cleaner to you.

Salesman   *You'll* sell the vacuum cleaner to *me*?

Housewife   Yes.

Salesman   OK. But it isn't as easy as you think.

Housewife   We'll see. Go inside and shut the door.

Salesman   All right.

The salesman goes into the house and closes the door. The housewife rings the bell. The salesman opens the door.

Salesman   Not today, thank you.

He closes the door. The housewife rings the bell again. The salesman opens the door again, and speaks in a high voice.

Salesman   Yes?

Housewife   Hello!

Salesman   Hello.

Housewife   My goodness me, what a beautiful house you've got!

Salesman   Ooh, do you like it?

Housewife   Like it? It's the most beautiful house I've seen for a long time.

Salesman   Thank you very much.

Housewife   May I come in?

Salesman   Er…

Housewife   Thank you. Oh, what a colourful carpet!

Salesman   Yes, it's lovely, isn't it?

Housewife   It's the most colourful carpet I've seen for ages. I should think it was very expensive.

Salesman   The most expensive one in the shop.

Housewife   And I suppose you've got a very good vacuum cleaner to look after it.

Salesman   A vacuum cleaner? No, I haven't.

Housewife   You haven't got a vacuum cleaner?

Salesman   No.

Housewife   Well, madam, this is your lucky day, because I have *here* the best vacuum cleaner that money can buy: the Superlative vacuum cleaner.

Salesman   Is it really good?

Housewife   Good? Good? It's the…the…

Salesman   (**In his own voice**) Quickest.

Housewife   …the quickest, the…

Salesman   Cleanest.

Housewife   …the cleanest, the cheapest, the smallest, the smartest, the most economical, the most effective, the most beautiful, the most revolutionary vacuum cleaner in the world.

Salesman   (**In a high voice again**) Ooh! How much is it?

Housewife   Just £65 to you, madam.

Salesman   I'll buy one.

Housewife   Good.

Salesman   (**In his own voice**) Er…where's the money?

Housewife   It's in my handbag on the kitchen table.

Salesman   Oh, right. (**In the high voice**) I'll just go and get some money.

He goes to the kitchen to get the money.

Housewife   Good idea, madam. You've made the right decision.

The salesman comes back, speaking in his own voice.

Salesman   Do you know, you're a fantastic saleswoman.

Housewife   Ooh!

Salesman   You've got a fantastic sales technique.

Housewife   Do you think so?

Salesman   Yes, you've got the best sales technique I've seen all day.

Housewife   Thank you!

Salesman   Thank *you*, madam.

He leaves and closes the door.

Salesman   (***Speaking to himself, counting the money***) Ten, twenty, thirty, forty, fifty, sixty, sixty-five. Now *that's* the way to sell a vacuum cleaner.

8 Superman and the psychiatrist

This sketch was first performed in 1975, and the text here is a shortened version of that used on stage. On stage, Superman achieved success as a pop star, singing with a rather intense electric guitarist and three dancing vocalists providing the accompaniment, the whole ensemble wearing shiny silver jackets. This ending has been modified here. (Superman, being a widely recognized figure, is a character we have used more than once in ETT sketches, as mentioned in the introductory note to Sketch 3, *The dentist*, in this book.)

Words and expressions

shout (vb.), *library*, *librarian*, *contract* (n.), *climb*, *lift* (vb.), *fly* (vb.), *trouble* (vb./n.) in *Sorry to trouble you* and *What seems to be the trouble?*

Note: rather than drawing attention to the words *library* and *librarian* or pre-teaching them if they are new words, you may like to let the students deduce their meaning from the context. This will avoid pre-empting the joke.

Preliminary practice

In the sketch, the psychiatrist gives some advice to the two patients, Mr Wilkins and Superman, using the expression *I think you should…*, so the preliminary practice could be based on this point.

Present the students with a series of problems or dilemmas, and ask them to come up with as many pieces of advice as they can for each one. Here are some problems or dilemmas to start with:
- I've just found £1000 in the street.
- The postman always reads my letters.
- My new shirt came to pieces in the washing-machine.

As the sketch involves Superman, you may also like to brainstorm the names of superheroes and see how much the class knows about them: for example, Superman has X-ray vision and can fly, etc.

Follow-up activities

① This activity, in which the students ask for and give advice in groups, is an extension of the preliminary practice. Each student has a problem or a dilemma written on a piece of paper. Here are two examples:

You are a police officer. You haven't got very much money, and you have a lot of debts. A criminal has offered you £5000 if you don't arrest him.
You are an architect. Someone has offered you a good job in another country. You will have to stay there for two years. You want to go, but your family don't.

The students take it in turns to explain their dilemma to the rest of their group, who offer advice, asking questions for more information, etc. as they think necessary. When all the students have had their turn, one student from each group could explain to the class their dilemma and the advice they received.

② Here is an activity for pairs of students. In the pairs, each student decides on a job. The jobs can be anything the students choose, but the activity is more entertaining if not *all* the jobs are conventionally 'exciting' ones (e.g. one student could be a librarian and the other a pop singer). Both dislike their jobs, and try to explain to the other the disadvantages of their own job and the advantages of the other's job. The pairs may like to re-enact their conversations for the whole class, avoiding actually *naming* the jobs and seeing if the rest of the class can guess what they are.

Props and costumes

For simple classroom re-enacting, all that is needed is a chair and desk for the psychiatrist, and another chair which is occupied successively by Mr Wilkins and Superman.

For a performance, it may be useful to have a telephone and some papers on the psychiatrist's desk. If a psychiatrist's couch rather than a chair is used for the patients, they should not remain lying down for long or the effect of their lines will be lost. Costumes: a white coat and perhaps glasses for the psychiatrist; possibly a white coat for the receptionist also; a costume – especially the T-shirt with the 'S' logo – for Superman; clothes as desired for Mr Wilkins.

Superman and the psychiatrist

Scene   A psychiatrist's consulting room
Characters   A psychiatrist
                Angela, the psychiatrist's receptionist
                Mr Wilkins
                Superman

The receptionist comes in.

Psychiatrist   Who's next, Angela?

Receptionist   There's a man to see you, doctor. His name is Wilkins. He says he can't talk quietly. He can only shout.

Mr Wilkins shouts from outside the door.

Mr Wilkins   Can I come in?!!

Psychiatrist   Hmm. Yes, I see. Ask him to come in.

Receptionist   Come in, Mr Wilkins.

Mr Wilkins   Thank you!!

He comes in. The receptionist goes out.

Mr Wilkins   Hello, doctor. Sorry to trouble you.

Psychiatrist   That's all right, Mr Wilkins. Do sit down.

Mr Wilkins sits down.

Psychiatrist   Now…what seems to be the trouble?

Mr Wilkins   Er…Well, doctor, I can't talk quietly. I can only shout.

Psychiatrist   (**Shouting**) How long have you been like this?

Mr Wilkins   Pardon?

Psychiatrist   (**Back to normal**) How long have you been like this?

Mr Wilkins   About a week.

Psychiatrist   Well, don't worry. I think you've got a very nice shouting voice.

Mr Wilkins   But I can't go on like this. I'll lose my job.

Psychiatrist   What *is* your job?

Mr Wilkins   I'm a librarian. I work in a library. I can't shout at work, you know.

Psychiatrist   In that case, Mr Wilkins, I think you should change your job.

Mr Wilkins   But what can I do? No one wants a man who can only shout!

Psychiatrist   You could get a job as an English teacher.

Mr Wilkins	An English teacher?
Psychiatrist	Yes, they shout all the time.
Mr Wilkins	All right, doctor. I'll do that. Goodbye.
Psychiatrist	Goodbye, Mr Wilkins.

He leaves, still shouting.

Mr Wilkins	Hey, you! Write down this verb!
Receptionist	Goodbye, Mr Wilkins.

The receptionist comes back into the room.

Receptionist	Is Mr Wilkins all right, doctor?
Psychiatrist	Yes. He's going to be an English teacher.
Receptionist	Oh.
Psychiatrist	Who's next?
Receptionist	Superman.
Psychiatrist	Superman?
Receptionist	Yes.
Psychiatrist	Oh, I see…someone who *thinks* he's Superman.
Receptionist	No, doctor. He really *is* Superman.
Psychiatrist	What? The big, strong man who flies through the air?
Receptionist	Yes.
Psychiatrist	Oh, I see. Ask him to come in.
Receptionist	Yes, doctor. (**To Superman**) Come this way, please.

Superman comes in, very tired and out-of-breath.

Superman	Thank you.
Psychiatrist	Thank you, Angela.

The receptionist goes out.

Psychiatrist	Good morning, Mr…er…
Superman	Superman.
Psychiatrist	Yes, Superman. Do sit down.

Superman sits down.

Superman	Thank you.
Psychiatrist	Well, what seems to be the trouble?
Superman	Well, doctor, I'm Superman. People think I can do everything, but I can't. I can't do *anything* any more.
Psychiatrist	What can't you do?

Superman	I can't climb buildings, I can't lift cars…and I can't fly.
Psychiatrist	Well, don't worry. A lot of people have that problem.
Superman	But you don't understand. I'm Superman. If you can't fly, you can't be Superman. It's in the contract.
Psychiatrist	Ah yes, I see.
Superman	In the old days, when people called for Superman, I could run into a telephone box, take off my boring grey city suit, and become Superman, all in ten seconds. Yesterday, I went into a telephone box, and it took me fifteen minutes just to take off my trousers. And when I came out, I couldn't remember where I was going. What do you think of that?

The psychiatrist is asleep.

Superman	Eh?
Psychiatrist	(**Waking up**) Er…What? Pardon?
Superman	What do you think?
Psychiatrist	I think you should change your job.
Superman	But what can I do?
Psychiatrist	Well, you've got a very nice face. You could be a pop singer.
Superman	A pop singer?
Psychiatrist	Yes, I can see it all now. Your name will be in lights! You'll be famous!
Superman	But I *am* famous. I'm *Superman.*
Psychiatrist	Not any more. From today, you are Rocky Superdazzle!
Superman	Do you think it's a good idea?
Psychiatrist	Yes, of course…Rocky.

The receptionist comes in again.

Receptionist	Doctor –
Psychiatrist	Yes, Angela?
Receptionist	– Mr Wilkins is back again.

Mr Wilkins comes in, shouting as before.

Mr Wilkins	Yes, I am. I've changed my mind. I don't want to be an English teacher. What else can I do?
Psychiatrist	Don't worry, Mr Wilkins. I've got another job for you. You can work with Rocky Superdazzle here.
Superman	How do you do?
Mr Wilkins	Rocky Superdazzle? That's not Rocky Superdazzle! That's Superman. I saw him in a telephone box yesterday. Superman! Huh! It took him fifteen minutes just to take off his trousers.
Psychiatrist	Well, he *was* Superman, but he's not Superman any more. I think you can both work together…

A few weeks later, at a pop concert.

Mr Wilkins   Ladies and gentlemen, you've heard of Rod Stewart! You've heard of Mick Jagger! You've heard of…Queen Elizabeth the Second of England! Well, tonight we present a new star on the pop scene. He's *sexier* than Rod Stewart! He's *wilder* than Mick Jagger! And he's…*taller* than Queen Elizabeth the Second of England! Ladies and gentlemen – Rocky Superdazzle!

The audience screams and applauds.

Superman   Thank you! Thank you very much! Thank you!

© Macmillan Publishers Limited 1995.

The lost property office

9

This sketch was first performed in 1982, and was initially prompted by the wish to write a sketch involving some language used in describing people or things. The version given here is very slightly condensed from the stage version, and the ending has been simplified: in the stage version, for the policeman's entrance, a rope was pulled in from the wings by the clerk (as if indeed an elephant were on the end of it), tied around the gangster's waist, and then pulled in further to reveal the policeman holding the other end.

Words and expressions

gangster, umbrella, elephant, circus, kilt, owner, traffic lights, fall asleep/wake up, generous, loving, bald, unusual

The expression *Kootchie-kootchie-koo!* is best described as 'baby-talk'.

Note the emphatic tone of the gangster's reply *I'd love to*, the formal tone of *Now, if you'd like to follow me…*, and the polite tone of the expressions *Not to worry, Sorry to have troubled you, Thank you for your help.*

Preliminary practice

Ask each student to think of an animal – it could be their favourite animal or an animal they find impressive – and to draw it on a piece of paper.

Ask all the students to make their animal special, unusual or distinctive in some way – an elephant with extra-long tusks, a cow wearing sun-glasses, or a squirrel playing the guitar, for example. (This is useful, since several students may well choose the same animal, and it also adds fun to the activity and allows the students to be imaginative.)

Put all the pieces of paper in a box, and ask each student in turn to take out one piece of paper and describe the animal shown on it. The other students listen to the descriptions and, for each one, try to guess who drew the picture.

Follow-up activities

① The students could devise a sketch of their own, like the original, but with the gangster inventing a different story about what he lost.

② As suggested in connection with Sketch 16 in Book 1, *A ticket to Birmingham*, the students (in pairs or groups) could complete the brief telephone conversations from the sketch, in which only the clerk's words are given. These are on page 4 of the sketch:

Hello? George?… It's Brenda…, *etc.*
Yes, George, I'm listening… Yes…, *etc.*
George… I want you to put a banana, *etc.*
George? George!… Get up, *etc.*
George, I think you should bring, *etc.*

The pairs or groups could take one or two different conversations each, or all the pairs/groups could have the same conversation(s).

The students should write out the clerk's words as given in the script, leaving a line for each reply (represented by three dots in the script), and then decide what George said. When they have completed their conversations, the pairs or groups could read them out to the rest of the class.

③ Individually, in pairs or groups, the students could give brief descriptions of famous people, whose identities the rest of the class then have to deduce.

Props and costumes

For simple classroom re-enacting, all that is needed is a table, two chairs, a sheet of paper (the form), a pen or pencil, and a telephone.

For a performance, the props noted above would be needed, and a large 'Lost Property Office' sign is also useful. Costumes: perhaps the classic outfit for the gangster (hat, dark shirt, light tie, jacket or mackintosh); a jacket or overall for the clerk; a uniform for the policeman. The gangster could wear dark glasses at the beginning, but should not keep them on throughout, as the face becomes less expressive if the eyes cannot be seen. The police sirens and the elephant noise can be made vocally off-stage.

The lost property office

Scene   A lost property office
Characters   The lost property office clerk
    A gangster
    A policeman

The gangster runs into the lost property office. There are police cars passing in the street at high speed.

Clerk   Can I help you?

Gangster   Where am I?

Clerk   You're in a lost property office.

Gangster   A lost property office?

Clerk   Yes. Have you lost something?

Gangster   Probably.

Clerk   What have you lost?

Gangster   I've lost my…umbrella.

Clerk   Ah, you want the Umbrella Section.

Gangster   The Umbrella Section?

Clerk   Yes. Go out into the street, turn left, and it's on the left.

Gangster   Into the street?

Clerk   Yes. You see, this isn't the Umbrella Section. This is the Animal Section.

Gangster   The Animal Section?

Clerk   Yes.

Gangster   In that case, I've lost my dog.

Clerk   You've lost your dog?

Gangster   Yes.

Clerk   Well, in that case, you want the *Small* Animal Section.

Gangster   The *Small* Animal Section?

Clerk   Yes. Go into the street, turn right, and it's on the right.

Gangster   Into the street?

Clerk   Yes. You see, this isn't the *Small* Animal Section. This is the *Large* Animal Section.

Gangster   The *Large* Animal Section?

Clerk   Yes.

Gangster   In that case, I've lost my elephant.

Clerk   You've lost your elephant?

Gangster	Yes.
Clerk	I see. Well, I'll need a few details. Would you like to sit down?
Gangster	I'd love to.

The gangster sits down.

Clerk	Now, first of all: Name.
Gangster	Er…Winston.
Clerk	Well, Mr Winston –
Gangster	No, *my* name isn't Winston. The elephant's name is Winston.
Clerk	I see. And what is *your* name?
Gangster	Churchill.
Clerk	(**Writing**) Churchill. Address?
Gangster	Er…Churchill's Circus.
Clerk	Oh, I see. It's a circus elephant.
Gangster	Is it?…Yes. Yes, it is!
Clerk	When did you last see him?
Gangster	Who?
Clerk	The elephant.
Gangster	Oh, Winston. Well, we were on a bus yesterday –
Clerk	On a bus?!
Gangster	Yes.
Clerk	How did Winston get on a bus?
Gangster	How did Winston get on a bus?
Clerk	Yes.
Gangster	That's a very good question. Well…He waited at the bus stop, and when the bus came along, he put out his arm. And when the bus stopped, he got on.
Clerk	I see. And then what happened?
Gangster	Well, we were upstairs on the bus –
Clerk	Upstairs?!
Gangster	Yes. Winston wanted to smoke a cigarette.
Clerk	A cigarette?!
Gangster	I know – I tell him every day: 'Winston, smoking is bad for you.' But he never listens.
Clerk	Hmm. What happened then?
Gangster	Well, I fell asleep.
Clerk	You fell asleep?
Gangster	Yes.
Clerk	I see. And then what happened?
Gangster	I don't know – I was asleep. But then I woke up, and Winston wasn't there.

Clerk   Hmm. Well, I'd better ask you a few questions about him. What kind of elephant is he?

Gangster   Oh, he's very nice – generous, loving…he likes collecting stamps.

Clerk   No – when I say 'What kind of elephant?', I mean: Is he an *African* elephant?

Gangster   Oh, no.

Clerk   So he's an *Indian* elephant.

Gangster   No.

Clerk   What kind of elephant is he?

Gangster   Scottish.

Clerk   A Scottish elephant?!

Gangster   Yes. He wears a kilt.

Clerk   I see. What colour is he?

Gangster   Colour? Well, he's elephant-coloured.

Clerk   And what colour is that?

Gangster   Blue.

Clerk   Blue?!

Gangster   It was very cold yesterday.

Clerk   Yes, it was. Next question: Colour of eyes.

Gangster   Well, you know, like an elephant.

Clerk   What colour is that?

Gangster   Red.

Clerk   Red?!

Gangster   Green.

Clerk   Green?!

Gangster   One red, one green.

Clerk   One red, one green?!

Gangster   Yes. We call him 'Traffic Lights'.

Clerk   I see. Colour of hair?

Gangster   Hair?

Clerk   Yes.

Gangster   He hasn't got any hair.

Clerk   I see. (**Writing**) Bald…So we're looking for a bald, blue, Scottish elephant, wearing a kilt and smoking a cigarette.

Gangster   Yes.

Clerk   Is there anything unusual about him?

Gangster   No, nothing at all.

Clerk   Good. Now, Mr Churchill, what should we do if we find Winston?

Gangster   Well…Put a banana in your hand, walk up to Winston, and say 'Kootchie-kootchie-koo'.

Clerk   What will Winston do?

Gangster Well, if it's Winston, he'll sit down and he'll eat the banana.

Clerk All right, Mr Churchill. Just wait a moment, and I'll call the Elephant Section.

Gangster Fine.

The clerk picks up the telephone and dials a number.

Clerk Hello? George?…It's Brenda…I'm fine, thank you – and you?…Good. George, have you got any elephants?…You haven't? Hold on a moment. (***To the gangster***) He hasn't got any elephants.

Gangster No elephants? Well, not to worry. Sorry to have troubled you. Thank you for your help. I'll be on my way. Goodbye.

He gets up. A police car passes in the street. He sits down again.

Gangster Er…Ask George to have another look.

Clerk All right. (***On the phone***) George, can you have another look?

Gangster Tell him to look under the table.

Clerk Look under the table…What?…(***To the gangster***) He's got one.

Gangster A table?

Clerk No, an *elephant*.

Gangster An *elephant*?

Clerk Yes. It was under the table.

Gangster Really?

Clerk (***On the phone***) Yes, George, I'm listening…Yes…Yes…Yes…Yes. Hold on. (***To the gangster***) He's got a bald, blue, Scottish elephant, wearing a kilt and smoking a cigarette. It sounds like Winston.

Gangster What about the banana?

Clerk Oh, yes. (***On the phone***) George…I want you to put a banana in your hand, and say 'Kootchie-kootchie-koo'…No, not to *me* – to the *elephant*. OK?…What?…Oh, no!

Gangster What's the matter?

Clerk The elephant sat down.

Gangster Good.

Clerk On George.

Gangster Tell George to give Winston the banana!

Clerk Right. (***On the phone***) George? George!…Get up and give the banana to the elephant…Hello?…What?…Oh, no!

Gangster What is it?

Clerk He's eaten the banana.

Gangster Who? Winston?

Clerk No. George.

Gangster Oh, no!

Clerk (***On the phone***) George, I think you should bring the elephant down here. The owner is waiting to take him away…OK…Bye.

The clerk puts down the telephone.

Clerk   Don't worry, Mr Churchill. Your elephant will be here in a moment.

Gangster   Look – before this elephant arrives, there's something you should know –

They hear the sound of an elephant.

Clerk   Ah, that must be Winston.

They hear the sound of someone falling over.

Clerk   And that's George.

Someone knocks at the door.

Clerk   Go on, Mr Churchill. Open the door.

Gangster   Oh, all right.

He opens the door.

Gangster   Hello, Winston. Kootchie-kootchie-koo!

Policeman   Mr Churchill?

Gangster   But…this isn't an elephant. It's a policeman.

Policeman   Very good, sir. Now, if you'd like to follow me…

Clerk   Goodbye, Mr Churchill. And don't forget: If you lose your elephant again, the Lost Property Office is here to help you.

Gangster   Oh, good. I'll remember that.

He leaves with the policeman.

The travel agency

10

Like Sketch 6, *Gussett and Rose*, in Book 1, this sketch began as a dialogue written for the Belgian magazine *English Pages*. It was adapted for the ETT's stage show, and first performed in 1975. In the stage version, the travel agent used a large number of visual aids, among them a rubber snake, a toy parachute and a reversible diagram of the Sahara Desert and the Atlantic Ocean, in order to illustrate the holidays he was offering; the script has therefore been slightly adapted for this book.

Words and expressions

fish and chip shop, parachute, map, sandstorm, snake, stampede (n.), *camel, bullfighting, exciting, dangerous, frightened, terrifying, wonderful, How about…?* and *What about…?* (used in making suggestions)

Various place-names and geographical terms occur in the sketch: *the Sahara Desert, the Arctic Ocean, the Amazon jungle, the Eiffel Tower, the London Underground, Spain, Paris* and *Brighton*.

Preliminary practice

Write each of the place-names and geographical terms listed above on an envelope, and put the envelopes on the board or a table. The individual students then each choose three of the places, and write, on small pieces of paper, an adjective to describe each of those places. (Encourage them to be imaginative about this; in other words, *hot* for the Sahara Desert and *cold* for the Arctic Ocean are a bit obvious.)

The students then place their pieces of paper in the relevant envelopes. Then invite students in turn to dip into an envelope and take out an adjective. If it is one of their own, they should say why they wrote, for example, *sad* about the Eiffel Tower; if it is someone else's, they can try to work out why that person wrote it and the person can then give their reason.

Follow-up activities

① The students could improvise conversations similar to the sketch. They could do this in pairs (travel agent and customer) or in threes (travel agent and two customers). The travel agents should try to sell a holiday which is strange and expensive; the customers should insist on the type of holiday *they* want. Cue-cards may be helpful; for example:

For the travel agent: *You are a travel agent. You have to sell holidays on the moon.*
And for the customer(s): *You want a skiing holiday in Scotland. Do not accept any other holiday.*

A variation: give each group a line – not obviously connected with holidays – which they must include in their conversation (e.g. *I've lost my glasses* or *My uncle grows his own vegetables*). The groups enact their conversations for the rest of the class, who try and identify these 'imposed' lines – believe it or not, they can be quite hard to spot!

② Give the students a few moments to think about the *best* holiday they have ever had and the *worst* holiday they have ever had. They can make brief notes if they like. Then they each have a maximum of one minute to speak: thirty seconds on their best holiday and thirty seconds on their worst holiday. They do not need to say anything very complicated: they could simply say when and where the holiday took place, who they were with, and what happened to make it good or bad.

Props and costumes

For classroom re-enacting, you will need: a chair and a desk for the travel agent; two chairs for the customers; a few travel brochures (or sheets of paper to represent them); a telephone; a pen or pencil, and a sheet of paper to represent the form.

For a performance, the props could simply be as noted for classroom re-enacting. You may, however, like to incorporate 'visual aids' such as those mentioned in the introductory note above, plus any or all of these: a toy camel, a toy gun, a toy boat, and an Underground map; the travel agent would hold them up at the relevant moments as he describes the holidays.

The travel agency

Scene	A travel agency in London
Characters	A travel agent
	Martin and Brenda Spencer

The travel agent is sitting at his desk in the travel agency. The phone rings.

Travel agent (**On the telephone**) Honest Harry's Happy Holidays. Can I help you?…Oh, it's *you*, sir…This *is* Perkins speaking, yes…The holidays in Brighton? Well, I haven't sold very many…I'm doing my best, but people aren't interested in Brighton these days…My job? Yes, I *do* like my job…Yes, I *do* want to *keep* my job…Yes, sir. All right, I'll sell some holidays in Brighton. Yes, sir. Yes, sir. Goodbye.

He puts the phone down.

Travel agent Oh, dear.

Martin and Brenda come in.

Martin Go on, Brenda.

Brenda Excuse me, is this a travel agency?

Travel agent No, madam. It's a fish and chip shop.

Brenda Oh, sorry. Come on, Martin.

Travel agent No, no, this *is* a travel agency. Just a little joke.

Brenda Oh.

Travel agent Yes, welcome to Honest Harry's Happy Holidays. Do sit down.

Brenda Thank you.

Martin Thank you.

They sit down.

Travel agent What can I do for you?

Brenda We'd like some information about holidays.

Travel agent Oh, good.

Martin Yes, we'd like to go somewhere interesting.

Travel agent Somewhere interesting? Have you been to Brighton?

Martin Brighton? No, we haven't –

Travel agent Really?

Brenda – and we don't want to, either.

Travel agent Why not?

Martin Well, it's not *exciting*. We want to go somewhere *exciting*.

Travel agent	Oh, I see. How about the Sahara Desert?
Brenda	The Sahara Desert?
Travel agent	Yes. Have you ever been there?
Martin	No, we haven't.
Travel agent	Well, this is the holiday for you. Forty-five days in the middle of the Sahara Desert.
Brenda	In the middle of the Sahara Desert? Is there anything to do?
Travel agent	Oh yes, there's plenty to do. Have you ever been in a sandstorm?
Martin	A sandstorm? No, we haven't.
Travel agent	Oh well, it's very exciting. There are sandstorms nearly every day. And lots of dangerous snakes. Have you ever been bitten by a dangerous snake?
Martin } **Brenda**	No!
Travel agent	Oh well, it's very exciting.
Brenda	No, I don't think we'd like –
Travel agent	Sandstorms, dangerous snakes, and, on the last day, a stampede of camels!
Martin	A stampede of camels? What's that?
Travel agent	Haven't you ever seen a stampede of camels?
Martin	No.
Travel agent	Oh, it's very exciting. You stand in the middle of three hundred camels, someone fires a gun in the air – Bang! – and all the camels get frightened and run away.
Brenda	With us standing in the middle?
Travel agent	Yes. Have you ever seen a frightened camel?
Brenda	No. Is it exciting?
Travel agent	Exciting? It's terrifying!
Martin	Isn't it dangerous?
Travel agent	Of course it's dangerous! That's what makes it exciting!
Martin	Er…how much is it?
Travel agent	£800.
Brenda	£800!
Travel agent	And £5 extra for the stampede of camels.
Brenda	That's very expensive.
Travel agent	Ah, I see. You want something cheaper. Um…how about the Arctic Ocean? Have you ever been to the Arctic?
Martin	No, we haven't.
Travel agent	Well, we can give you three weeks in a small boat in the Arctic Ocean. Each boat has a small hole in the bottom –
Brenda	A hole in the bottom?
Travel agent	– and you have enough food for ten days.
Martin	Ten days?

Travel agent	That's right.
Martin	But the holiday is for three weeks.
Travel agent	That's what makes it exciting! And it's only £600.
Brenda	£600! It's still much too expensive for us.
Martin	Have you got anything a little bit cheaper?
Travel agent	Cheaper…well, I don't know. Let me see…Um…Oh, yes. Now *this* is a holiday to remember. The Amazon jungle. Have you been to the Amazon jungle?
Martin	No, we haven't.
Travel agent	Well, this may be the holiday for you. We drop you into the middle of the Amazon jungle by parachute –
Martin	By parachute!
Travel agent	Yes, we drop you into the middle of the Amazon jungle, with a map –
Brenda	Well, at least you get a map.
Travel agent	– with a map of the London Underground.
Brenda	Oh. I don't think we'd like that. It sounds very dangerous.
Travel agent	Yes, but it's very *exciting*! This is the twentieth century. People want exciting holidays. *You* said *you* wanted an exciting holiday.
Martin	But all your holidays are dangerous, expensive, and too far away from home.
Travel agent	Oh, I see. Now you want something nearer home.
Martin	Er…yes.
Travel agent	Have you ever been to Spain?
Martin	No, we haven't.
Travel agent	We can offer you a month, fighting the strongest bulls in Spain.
Brenda	Bullfighting? No, I don't want to do that.
Travel agent	Oh. Have you ever been to Paris?
Martin	No, we haven't.
Travel agen	What about ten days in Paris?…
Martin	That sounds marvellous!
Travel agent	…painting the outside of the Eiffel Tower.
Brenda **Martin**	} No, thanks!
Travel agent	Well, what about two weeks in Brighton?
Brenda	No, thanks!
Martin	Just a minute. Did you say 'Brighton'?
Travel agent	Yes. How about two weeks in Brighton, staying in a nice quiet hotel by the sea?
Brenda	Well, yes…
Martin	Yes, that sounds wonderful!
Travel agent	It's not very exciting. No camels, no snakes, but you can't have everything, can you?
Brenda	No. That's very nice. We'll take it.

Martin	How much is it?
Travel agent	£50 each, please. Could you just sign this form for the reservations?

He gives Martin a form.

Travel agent	Just here, please.

Martin signs.

Travel agent	Thank you. And here. And here. And here. And… here. Thank you.
Brenda	Thank you very much.
Martin	Goodbye.
Travel agent	Goodbye, and I hope you enjoy your holiday.

Martin and Brenda leave. The telephone rings.

Travel agent	(**On the telephone**) Honest Harry's Happy Holidays. Can I help you?… Well, we've got some very nice holidays in Brighton, as a matter of fact…

© Macmillan Publishers Limited 1995.

11 Gerry Brown's driving test

This sketch was first performed in 1976. (In the initial version, the sketch resolved with the examiner falling for Gerry and awarding him a pass in his test; this ending was subsequently revised.) On stage, the car is represented by four chairs, and everything is done in mime: the climbing in and out of the car, the driving along, turning, stopping, and so on, accompanied by vocal noises for the engine. The script has been slightly altered for this book: a great deal of confusion over seating in the car has been omitted, and the ending has been shortened somewhat.

Words and expressions

examiner, brain surgeon, glasses (= spectacles), *traffic lights, the big day* (= the day on which something important is going to happen), *more or less the same; just in case*

Note the idiomatic use of *she* to refer to an aeroplane in Gerry's exclamation *Up she goes!*, and also the formal tone of Gerry's offer to the examiner: *Allow me to open the door for you.*

Preliminary practice

Elicit and write on the board the sequence of actions involved in starting and driving a car, for example, *turn the ignition key, briefly press the accelerator, put your foot on the clutch, put the car in first gear, release the handbrake, look in the mirror, indicate, drive away.*

Then ask a few individual students in turn to sit in front of the class and mime the sequence of actions as the other students call out the instructions.

Then other individual students in turn can mime the sequence, missing out one action. The rest of the class should watch, remaining silent until the end of the mime each time. When the the mime is completed, they should indicate what the omission was: for example, *She/He didn't look in the mirror* or *She/He should have looked in the mirror before she/he drove away.*

Follow-up activities

① The students, in pairs, could do some more 'driving' mimes, expanding on those from the preliminary practice. Two students sit side by side, Student **A** being a driver and Student **B** a driving examiner (or driving instructor). **B** gives instructions and makes comments, and **A** reacts as appropriate in mime. The instructions and comments can be those from the sketch (*Drive the car straight down the road; Turn right; Turn left; The traffic lights are red*), plus any others which **B** can think of (e.g. *Park over there; Go a little faster; Stop outside that house; Put the car into reverse,* etc.). If **A** executes an instruction wrongly, **B** should comment on this.

② Divide the class into groups and give each group a picture of a road sign. Each group then invents a meaning for their road sign which is incorrect but 'plausible'; e.g. for the signs below, these meanings could be, respectively: *Umbrellas must be carried; Danger: sausages in road* and *No boomerangs.* The groups then show their signs to the rest of the class, giving their invented meanings. The rest of the class give the correct meanings, which for the signs below are: *Roadworks ahead* (or 'Men working on the road', etc.); *Roundabout* (or 'There's a roundabout ahead', etc.) and *No right turn* (or 'You can't turn right', etc.).

Props and costumes

For simple classroom re-enacting, all that is required is four chairs, arranged to represent the car; the examiner may like to have a pen and a clipboard with papers on it.

For a performance, similarly, four chairs will represent the car, and the pen and clipboard are useful for the examiner. Costumes can be as desired: possibly something that suggests an old-fashioned aviator for Gerry, and something quite smart for the examiner. Gerry should have a pair of glasses (which he has in his pocket until they are needed).

Gerry Brown's driving test

Scene	A car
Characters	Gerry Brown
	Brian Smith, Gerry's friend
	A driving examiner

Brian has just arrived at the test centre in his car. He is sitting in it, waiting for Gerry.

Brian Hmm…Three o'clock. Where is he?…Ah, there he is. Gerry! Gerry!

Gerry comes to the car.

Gerry Ah, hello!

Brian Hello, Gerry.

Brian gets out of the car.

Brian Well, the big day, eh?

Gerry Yes, my driving test. It's very good of you to lend me your car.

Brian Oh, that's all right, Gerry. You *have* had driving lessons, haven't you?

Gerry Oh, yes. Well…I had *one*.

Brian One?

Gerry Yes. I had one last night. It was very good.

Brian That's not enough. You should have had at least *ten*!

Gerry Now don't worry. I've flown aeroplanes, you know, and it's all more or less the same. You just jump in, switch on, and up she goes!

Brian Yes, but this isn't an *aeroplane*. It's a car. *My* car!

Gerry Oh yes, I can see that.

Brian Hmm…*that's* another problem.

Gerry What?

Brian Your eyes.

Gerry What's the matter with my eyes?

Brian Well, they're not exactly perfect, are they?

Gerry Well, I know I can't see very well, but –

Brian But you told the authorities that your eyes were perfect. You shouldn't have done that.

Gerry Yes, I know. But don't worry, everything will be all right. I borrowed these glasses from my uncle, and he says they're marvellous.

Brian Your *uncle's* glasses! But Gerry, you should have brought your *own* glasses.

Gerry   I haven't got any of my own. But don't worry, my uncle has worn these for twenty-five years, and he's a brain surgeon.

Brian   Gerry –

Gerry   Look, I'll put them on.

He puts on the glasses.

Gerry   There. Oh…Um…Brian?…Brian?

He bumps into the car.

Gerry   Oh.

Brian   Gerry, look, here comes the examiner.

Gerry   Oh yes, I see. He looks like a very nice man.

Brian   Gerry, it's not a *man*. It's a *woman*.

Gerry   Oh.

Brian   Now listen, Gerry. There's only one way you can pass this test.

Gerry   Yes?

Brian   Be polite.

Gerry   Be polite and –

Brian   Shh, Gerry. Here she is.

The examiner arrives.

Examiner   Mr Brown?

Gerry   Er…yes.

Examiner   I'm the examiner. Shall we get in?

Gerry   Er…yes. Allow me to open the door for you.

He opens the door and the examiner gets into the car.

Examiner   Thank you.

He closes the door.

Gerry   Was that all right?

Brian   Very good, Gerry. But I think I'll come with you, just in case.

Gerry   All right.

Gerry and Brian get into the car. Brian sits in the back.

Examiner   Now, Mr Brown. I'd like you to drive the car straight down the road.

Gerry   Straight down the road. Yes.

He tries to drive away. The car stalls.

Gerry   Oh. Sorry.

He tries again, and drives away very fast.

Examiner	Turn right, Mr Brown.

Gerry turns left.

Brian	Gerry! You turned *left*. She said 'Right'. You should have turned *right*.
Gerry	(**Cheerfully**) Sorry!
Examiner	Turn left, Mr Brown.

Gerry turns right.

Brian	Gerry! You turned *right*. You should have turned *left*.
Examiner	The traffic lights are red, Mr Brown.
Brian / **Examiner**	Red!

Gerry stops the car at the traffic lights.

Gerry	Ha, ha! Very good, eh? Straight on?
Examiner	Er…n-n-no, Mr Brown. I think I'll get out here.
Gerry	Oh. Allow me to open the door for you.
Examiner	No, no, thank you. That won't be necessary.

She gets out of the car and walks away.

Examiner	I should have stayed in bed today. I knew it…I knew it was going to be a bad day.
Gerry	Oh, dear.
Brian	I told you you should have had more lessons, Gerry.
Gerry	Ah, green!

Gerry drives away very fast.

Brian	Gerry! Gerry! Slow down, Gerry! Gerry!!

© Macmillan Publishers Limited 1995.

12 Giovanni's café

This sketch was first performed in 1975. The idea came from the thought that there are a lot of humorous possibilities in the situation where two people who want to be alone – for example at a café table – are interrupted by a third person. The stage version in fact consisted of *two* sketches, the first set in Paris, with only Geoffrey and Dorothy, and the second (coming later in the show) set in Rome, and involving all four characters. The version here is a combination of elements from both these sketches.

Words and expressions

romantic, innocent, remarkable, magnificent, honest, honeymoon, statue, kindergarten, telephone-box, we haven't got a care in the world (= we haven't got any worries); *all the time in the world* (= lots of time), *May I sit here?* (more formal than *Can I sit here?*)

Note the expressions *Delighted to meet you* (used when meeting someone) and *Delighted to have met you* (used when leaving someone after a first meeting), both of which Teresa says very coldly.

Preliminary practice

Ask the students, in pairs or groups, to think of the most *romantic* holiday they can imagine. They should make a note of the location, the season, the means of transport to get there, and any other details they like. Then invite each group to tell the rest of the class what they have decided. Then, as a plenary activity, ask the students to think of the most *embarrassing* thing that could happen during such a romantic holiday.

If you feel that your students are too young for this activity, you could simply brainstorm what to say when wanting to join people you don't know at a café table or in a train compartment, for example (*May I sit here?, Do you mind if I sit here?, Is this seat taken?,* etc.), and then have the students practise some short exchanges using those expressions.

Follow-up activities

① The general shape of the sketch is this: Two people (**A** and **B**) are joined by a third (**C**) who knew **B** some time ago; they discuss their reasons for being in the city they are in and the circumstances in which **B** and **C** knew one another. The students could improvise similar conversations based on cue-cards such as these:

*Card for **A** and **B*:* You are an engaged couple. You are on holiday in Paris. Your names are Tom Johnson and Alice Brown. Tom knew Brian Williams at school.
*Card for **C*:* Your name is Brian Williams. You are an engineer. You are in Paris for a business meeting. You knew Tom Johnson at school.

Or:

*Card for **A** and **B*:* You are a grandmother and grandson. You are on holiday in Athens. Your names are Martha Green and Jack Green. Martha used to work with Diana Walker.
*Card for **C*:* Your name is Diana Walker. You are a retired nurse. You are in Athens visiting some friends. You used to work with Martha Green.

② In the sketch, Geoffrey tries several times to change the subject of the conversation: *Look at that remarkable statue!; I think we'd better go,* etc. The students could try something similar, one person attempting to explain something to another (or tell them a joke, for example), while a third makes constant attempts to change the subject.

Props and costumes

For simple classroom re-enacting, a table with three chairs at it is all that is required.

For a more elaborate performance, the table could have on it a bright café tablecloth and miscellaneous objects (e.g. a menu, containers for salt, pepper, sugar, etc.). Costumes: Geoffrey and Dorothy could have sunglasses – although not worn throughout, as hiding the eyes makes the face less expressive – and perhaps cameras, as accessories to their casual holiday wear; Teresa should also be in summer clothes; Giovanni could have an apron or short waiter's jacket, and perhaps a tray.

Giovanni's café

Scene   A pavement café in Rome
Characters   Geoffrey Burton
Dorothy Burton, Geoffrey's wife
Teresa Pilkington
Giovanni

Geoffrey and Dorothy are sitting at a table in front of the café.

Geoffrey   Well, here we are in Rome. The sun is shining, and we haven't got a care in the world.

Dorothy   Yes, Rome is so beautiful.

Geoffrey   And it's such a beautiful day.

Dorothy   This square looks lovely in the sunshine.

Geoffrey   And it's so nice, sitting here with you. No trains to catch…

Dorothy   No telephones to answer…

Geoffrey   No boring business people to talk to…Do you know, this is the first holiday we've had for five years – since we were married.

Dorothy   And it's our first visit to Rome, too. It's like a second honeymoon.

Geoffrey   Yes, and now we're alone together, with all the time in the world.

Dorothy   Yes.

Geoffrey   Just you, and me, and romantic Rome.

Dorothy   Yes.

Teresa comes to their table.

Teresa   Excuse me, do you speak English?

Geoffrey   Yes.

Teresa   May I sit here?

Geoffrey   Er…oh…yes.

Teresa sits down.

Teresa   Thank you. Just a minute – it's Geoffrey – Geoffrey Burton!

Geoffrey   Good God! Teresa Pilkington!

Teresa   Geoffrey, darling! How lovely to see you! It's been so long since we –

Geoffrey   Er…Teresa, this is my *wife*, Dorothy.

Teresa   Oh, your wife. Delighted to meet you.

Dorothy   So you know Geoffrey, do you?

Teresa   Oh yes, Geoffrey and I are old friends, aren't we, Geoffrey?

Geoffrey	No. Er…yes. Er…what are you doing in Rome, Teresa?
Dorothy	You're old friends, are you?
Teresa	Oh yes, I've known Geoffrey for years and years, since we were both young and innocent.
Geoffrey	Goodness me! Look at that remarkable statue!
Dorothy	Geoffrey!…Tell me, Miss Pilkington, what exactly do you mean by 'young and innocent'?
Teresa	Well, darling, before Geoffrey met me, he was just an innocent boy.
Geoffrey	Er…yes…we met at kindergarten.
Teresa	Oh, Geoffrey, you know that's not what I mean.
Dorothy	Well, what exactly *do* you mean?
Geoffrey	Good Lord! Look at that magnificent telephone box!
Dorothy	Geoffrey!
Geoffrey	Well, you don't see telephone boxes like that in England, do you?
Teresa	Poor Geoffrey! Before he met me, his life was so boring. He was a student at an awful college in the mountains, and he hated every minute of it.
Dorothy	But Geoffrey – you told me you *loved* that college in the mountains!
Teresa	Oh yes, that's because he met *me* there.
Dorothy	What – at the college?
Teresa	No, in the mountains.
Geoffrey	Er, Dorothy, I think we'd better go. The Colosseum closes at six o'clock, you know.
Dorothy	Sit down, Geoffrey. It's only half past eleven.
Teresa	Yes, I remember that day so well – the day that we met. The mountains were so beautiful, the sky was so blue –
Dorothy	– and Geoffrey was so *green*, I suppose.
Teresa	'Green'? What do you mean?
Dorothy	'Green.' Young and innocent. Just the way you like them, I suppose.
Teresa	Well, really!

Teresa gets up.

Teresa	Excuse me!…Goodbye, Geoffrey. (**Sarcastically**) Delighted to have met you, Mrs Burton.
Geoffrey	Teresa…um…
Teresa	Goodbye, Geoffrey.

Teresa leaves.

Geoffrey	Oh, dear.
Dorothy	So before you met her, you were just an innocent boy! You told me I was the first woman in your life, and I believed you…and *I've* been *so* honest with *you*.
Geoffrey	Yes, Dorothy.
Dorothy	I've told you everything.

Geoffrey	Yes, Dorothy, I know. I was the first man in your life.
Dorothy	The first and *only* man, Geoffrey.

Giovanni comes to the table.

Geoffrey	Oh…waiter. I'll have a Martini, please.
Giovanni	Certainly, sir. And for you, madam? Oh! Dorothy!
Dorothy	Giovanni!
Giovanni	Dorothy!
Geoffrey	Giovanni?
Giovanni	Dorothy, it's wonderful to see you again!
Geoffrey	Dorothy, have you met this man before?
Dorothy	Well, Geoffrey –
Giovanni	Dorothy, it must be five years!
Dorothy	Six, Giovanni, six!
Giovanni	And now you've come back to Rome!
Geoffrey	Come back? What's he talking about?
Dorothy	Well, Geoffrey –
Giovanni	Come with me, Dorothy. We've got *so* much to talk about!
Dorothy	Oh…er, yes…um…excuse me, Geoffrey.

Giovanni and Dorothy leave.

Geoffrey	Dorothy! Dorothy!

13 Shakespeare's house

This sketch was first performed in 1974. (The idea came from an example used by one of the ETT members in a lesson concerning the use of *must/can't (be)...* and *must/can't have (been)...* for making deductions about present and past situations.) We have adapted it slightly for this book, but the 'plot' remains the same as the stage version. We were originally going to include more quotations from Shakespeare, but in the end stuck to just the most well-known one of all, 'To be or not to be...'.

Words and expressions

tragedy (= type of play), *furniture, armchair, ashtray, typewriter, tape-recorder, microphone, souvenir, grandson, There must be some mistake* (= I believe there is a misunderstanding here), *disturb* (in *I hope we haven't disturbed you too much*)

The quotation 'To be, or not to be – that is the question' is from *Hamlet*, Act III, Scene I.

Preliminary practice

Here is an activity to practise deductions using *must be* and *must have been*. Write on the board, jumbled up, the first names, family names, nationalities and occupations of three famous living people; for example:

BILL   LENNOX   FRENCH   POLITICIAN
ERIC   CLINTON   SCOTTISH   SOCCER PLAYER
ANNIE   CANTONA   AMERICAN   SINGER

In groups, the students make sentences such as *We think Bill Lennox is a Scottish soccer player.* Keep inviting sentences until the correct identities of two people have been established; then you can say, for example, 'So Annie Lennox *must be* a Scottish singer.'

The same exercise using three famous people who are no longer alive will result in a sentence with *must have been.*

Follow-up activities

The preliminary practice, and the sketch itself, provided examples of deductions using *must (be)*, *must have (been)*, etc. Here is another activity involving deductions, in which the students attempt to solve a crime. If they think they know the answer, they should express their ideas using *must*, and other students can challenge them.

A robbery has taken place in an old man's flat in a small block. Draw a diagram on the board, like this:

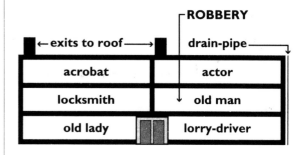

Two students choose roles from the five suspects above, e.g. the actor and the acrobat. They leave the room and jointly prepare their alibi (where they were at the time of the robbery, what they were doing, etc.). The rest of the class prepare questions and then act as detectives, questioning the two suspects individually; this may reveal inconsistencies in the alibis. The class should then give their conclusions, e.g. *It must have been the actor* or *The acrobat must have done it.*

Props and costumes

For classroom re-enacting, it is useful to have a table and chair to refer to in the early part of the sketch, and a newspaper for the man to remain behind until he is woken up; a typewriter and an ashtray (or objects to represent them) and some pieces of paper (to represent the money) are also useful.

For a more elaborate performance, you will need some furniture, including a chair or armchair for the man, and the typewriter, ashtray and newspaper. It is not necessary to have a television on stage – in our stage version, it was always indicated by the actors as being in the audience. The tourists could have cameras and perhaps sunglasses (although not worn throughout, hiding their eyes).

Shakespeare's house

Scene   The living-room of a house in Stratford-upon-Avon, the town where Shakespeare was born

Characters   Sidney and Ethel, tourists

A man

Sidney and Ethel come into the room.

Sidney   Well, Ethel, here we are in Shakespeare's front room. This must be where he wrote all his famous tragedies.

Ethel   I'm not surprised, with furniture like this.

Sidney   What do you mean?

Ethel   Well, look at that armchair. He can't have been comfortable, sitting there.

Sidney   Don't be silly! He probably sat at this table when he was writing tragedies.

Ethel   Oh, yes…Look!

She shows Sidney a typewriter.

Ethel   This must be Shakespeare's typewriter.

Sidney   Shakespeare's typewriter?

Ethel   Yes. He must have written all his plays on this.

Sidney   Ethel! That can't be Shakespeare's typewriter.

Ethel   Why not?

Sidney   Because Shakespeare didn't *use* a typewriter.

Ethel   Didn't he?

Sidney   No, of course he didn't. He was a very busy man. He didn't have time to sit in front of a typewriter all day. He probably used a tape-recorder.

Ethel   A tape-recorder?

Sidney   Yes. I can see him now. He must have sat on this chair, holding his microphone in his hand, saying: 'To be, or not to be.'

Ethel   What does that mean?

Sidney   Ah well, that is the question.

Ethel   Sidney, look!

Sidney   What?

Ethel   Over here. This must be Shakespeare's television.

Sidney   Shakespeare's television?

Ethel   Yes, it must be. It looks quite old.

Sidney   Shakespeare didn't have a *television*.

Ethel   Why not?

Sidney Why not? Because he went to the theatre every night. He didn't have time to sit at home, watching television.

Ethel Oh.

They hear someone snoring.

Ethel Sidney, what's that? I can hear something. Oh, look!

Sidney Where?

Ethel Over there. There's a man over there, behind the newspaper. I think he's asleep.

Sidney Oh, yes. He must be one of Shakespeare's family. He's probably Shakespeare's grandson.

Ethel Ooh!

Sidney I'll just go and say 'Hello'.

He goes over to the man and shouts.

Sidney Hello!

Man What? Eh? What's going on?

Sidney Good morning.

Man Good mor– Who are you?

Ethel We're tourists.

Man Tourists?

Sidney Yes.

Ethel It must be very interesting, living here.

Man Interesting? Living here? What are you talking about?

Sidney Well, it must be interesting, living in a famous house like this.

Man Famous house?

Ethel Yes, there must be hundreds of people who want to visit Shakespeare's house.

Man Shakespeare's house? Look, there must be some mistake.

Sidney This *is* Shakespeare's house, isn't it?

Man *This* is Number 34, Railway Avenue…and *I* live here!

Ethel Yes. You must be Shakespeare's grandson.

Man Shakespeare's grandson?

Ethel Yes.

Sidney Ethel! Look at this!

Ethel What is it?

Sidney Look at it!

He is holding an ashtray.

Ethel Ooh, Shakespeare's ashtray!

Sidney Yes, William Shakespeare's ashtray! Mr Shakespeare, I would like to buy this ashtray as a souvenir of our visit to your grandfather's house.

© Macmillan Publishers Limited 1995.

Man	For the last time, my name is not –
Sidney	I'll give you ten pounds for it.
Man	Now listen…Ten pounds?
Sidney	All right then – twenty pounds.
Man	Twenty pounds for that ashtray?
Ethel	Well, it *was* William Shakespeare's ashtray, wasn't it?
Man	William Shakespeare's…Oh, yes, of course. William Shakespeare's ashtray.

Sidney gives the man twenty pounds.

Sidney	Here you are. You're sure twenty pounds is enough…
Man	Well…
Sidney	All right then. Twenty-five pounds.

He gives the man another five pounds.

Man	Thank you. And here's the ashtray.

The man gives Sidney the ashtray.

Sidney	Thank you very much.
Ethel	I hope we haven't disturbed you too much.
Man	Oh, not at all. I always enjoy meeting people who know such a lot about Shakespeare. Goodbye.
Ethel	Goodbye.

Ethel and Sidney leave.

14 Mr Universe

This sketch was first performed in 1980. The version in this book is slightly different from the version used on stage: in the stage version, there were *four* contestants in the competition, the first of them being a member of the audience; after all the contestants had been seen, the audience chose the winner, who always – unsurprisingly – turned out to be the first contestant, the audience-member. This winner was then rewarded with an ETT souvenir, while the three losing contestants were involved in a song.

Words and expressions

contestant, judges, votes, congratulations, fantastic, incredible, amazing, fascinating, sensational, ambition, hobby(ies), free time, unemployed, What do you do? (= What's your job?), *Really?* (showing interest in something someone has said); *quite* (for emphasis, in *that's quite enough*)

Note the exaggerated tone of *Windows are my life!*, the rude and abrupt tone of *All right, get on with it!* and the ironic tone of *That was fascinating*.

Preliminary practice

Here is an activity to prepare the students for the kind of interviews they will hear in the sketch.

Put the class into pairs. In each pair, one student is a famous person, the other a journalist. In their pairs, the students decide who their famous person is. Then – quietly, so that other pairs can't overhear them – the pairs of students prepare their interviews. In the interviews, the celebrities' *names* should not be mentioned, but they should be questioned about their life, their work, etc. (For example, if the famous person were Steven Spielberg, the interview might include: *Why are you here in Italy? – I've come to talk about my new film*, etc.) The pairs then perform their interviews in turn for the rest of the class, who work out the identity of each famous person.

Follow-up activities

① The students could devise a sketch of their own, along the same lines as the original, but with different contestants in the competition, i.e. characters with different jobs, hobbies and ambitions.

② The students could do a class survey on the subjects of *Hobbies, Jobs* (actual or desired for the future) and *Ambitions*. The class could be divided into three groups, with each of the groups responsible for one of the subject areas. The members of the groups then (inside or outside class) gather information from all the members of the class about the relevant area, and arrange this information in tables, lists, categories, etc. When this work has been completed, the groups' spokespersons present the results of their surveys to the class as a whole.

③ Individual students, or pairs or groups, each think of a job. The other students try to find out what the job is by asking questions. The questions must be of the type which can be answered with *Yes* or *No*. For example, *Do you work indoors?, Do you work outdoors?, Do you work in a shop?, Do you work in an office?, Do you earn a lot of money?, Do you work with animals?*, etc. There could be a limit on the number of questions which can be asked (as in the traditional game of 'Twenty Questions'); if the job has not been guessed within that number of questions, it is then revealed.

Props and costumes

For classroom re-enacting, no props are really necessary, although Gloria may like to have something to represent a microphone (e.g. a pen or rolled paper) and three small pieces of card.

For a performance, the following props are useful: the microphone – although it does not have to be plugged in – and cards for Gloria; a bucket and sponge for Arnold, and a piece of paper for his poem (perhaps unfolded or unrolled to great length on the line 'There's a bit more'); a large sign reading 'The Mr Universe Competition'. Costumes: possibly something 'sparkly' for Gloria to coincide with her family name; an overall for Arnold; short trousers for Elvis; clothes as desired for Ernest.

Mr Universe

Scene	The 'Mr Universe' competition
Characters	Gloria Sparkle, the presenter
	Arnold Higgins
	Elvis Smith } the contestants
	Ernest Bottom

The competition is just beginning.

Gloria Yes, ladies and gentlemen, it's time once again for the 'Mr Universe' competition – the competition to find the most *fantastic*, the most *incredible*, the most *amazing* man in the world. Who will be this year's Mr Universe? Our three judges will decide. But first let's meet the contestants. Contestant number one – Arnold Higgins!

Arnold Higgins enters, carrying a bucket and a sponge.

Gloria Ladies and gentlemen, this is Arnold Higgins.

Arnold Hello!

Gloria (***Reading from a card in her hand***) Arnold is 63 years old.

Arnold What? No, no, no. 36, not 63.

Gloria Sorry, Arnold.

Arnold That's all right.

Gloria Arnold is 36 years old. Tell me, Arnold – what do you do?

Arnold I'm a window cleaner.

Gloria He's a window cleaner, ladies and gentlemen! And tell me, Arnold – how long have you been a window cleaner?

Arnold Well, Gloria, I'm 36 now, and I started cleaning windows when I was 33. So I've been cleaning windows for…er…

Gloria Three years?

Arnold Yes. How did you know?

Gloria It's written on this card. Do you like it?

Arnold looks at the card.

Arnold Yes. It's a very nice card.

Gloria No, no – not the card. Do you like cleaning windows?

Arnold Do I like cleaning windows?

Gloria Yes.

Arnold Do *I* like cleaning windows?

Gloria Yes.

Arnold Do I like *cleaning* windows?

Gloria	Yes.
Arnold	No! I don't *like* cleaning windows – I *love* it!
Gloria	You love it.
Arnold	Yes, I love it. Big windows, small windows, broken windows –
Gloria	Yes, I see.
Arnold	Windows are my life! I've cleaned windows all over the world.
Gloria	Really?
Arnold	Yes. Do you know Buckingham Palace?
Gloria	Yes.
Arnold	Do you know the *windows* of Buckingham Palace?
Gloria	Yes. Arnold, have *you* cleaned the windows of Buckingham Palace?
Arnold	No – but I'd like to.
Gloria	Ah, so your *ambition* is to clean the windows of Buckingham Palace.
Arnold	Yes.
Gloria	Thank you, Arnold.

She wants Arnold to go.

Arnold	Before I go, I'd like to tell you about my hobby.
Gloria	What's that, Arnold?
Arnold	My hobby is writing poetry. I'd like to read one of my poems.
Gloria	Oh.
Arnold	It's about windows.
Gloria	Ah.
Arnold	(**Reading**) 'Oh, windows! Oh, windows! Oh, windows!'
Gloria	Oh, no!
Arnold	'Windows, windows, big and small! Windows, windows, I love you all!'
Gloria	Thank you, Arnold.
Arnold	There's a bit more.
Gloria	No, thank you, Arnold – that's quite enough. Ladies and gentlemen, the first contestant: Arnold Higgins!

Arnold leaves.

Gloria	Now let's meet the second contestant, who also wants to be this year's Mr Universe!

Elvis Smith enters. He is wearing short trousers and is rather shy.

Elvis	Er…Hello.
Gloria	What is your name?
Elvis	Elvis.

Gloria	Elvis?
Elvis	Yes. Elvis Smith.
Gloria	How old are you, Elvis?
Elvis	42.
Gloria	And what do you do?
Elvis	Nothing. I'm still at school.
Gloria	Still at school?
Elvis	Yes.
Gloria	What do you want to do when you leave school?
Elvis	Go to university.
Gloria	I see. And what is your hobby, Elvis?
Elvis	My hobby?
Gloria	Yes. What do you like doing in your free time?
Elvis	Oh well, I like meeting people. Hello, Gloria.
Gloria	Hello, Elvis.
Elvis	And I like fishing.
Gloria	Yes?
Elvis	And swimming.
Gloria	Thank you, Elvis.
Elvis	And collecting stamps, and playing football, and dancing –
Gloria	Thank you, Elvis.
Elvis	And climbing mountains, and water-skiing, and boxing –
Gloria	*Thank you, Elvis!* Ladies and gentlemen, Elvis Smith!

Elvis leaves.

Gloria	Well, ladies and gentlemen, that was Elvis Smith. Now let's meet the last contestant. From Liverpool: Ernest Bottom!

Ernest Bottom enters. He is not very friendly.

Gloria	Well, Ernest, it's wonderful to have you here –
Ernest	All right, get on with it!
Gloria	Oh. Well…Ernest, would you like to answer a few questions?
Ernest	No.
Gloria	Oh, come on, Ernest!
Ernest	All right – just a few.
Gloria	Thank you. Tell me – what do you do?
Ernest	What do I do?
Gloria	Yes.

Ernest Nothing. I'm unemployed.

Gloria Oh.

Ernest I used to be a bus driver.

Gloria Did you?

Ernest Yes. But I lost my job.

Gloria Why?

Ernest I can't drive.

Gloria Oh, I see. What do you like doing in your free time?

Ernest Nothing.

Gloria Oh, come on, Ernest! Haven't you got any hobbies?

Ernest Well…I've got one. I like gardening. Shall I tell you about my garden?

Gloria Yes!

Ernest Well…it's…

Gloria Yes?

Ernest It's…

Gloria Yes?

Ernest It's green!

Gloria sighs.

Gloria Well, thank you, Ernest. That was fascinating. Ladies and gentlemen, Ernest Bottom.

Ernest leaves.

Gloria Well, now we've met the three contestants, and our judges are ready with their votes. For Arnold Higgins: *one* vote. For Elvis Smith: *one* vote. And for Ernest Bottom: *one* vote. Well, this is sensational, ladies and gentlemen! This year, we have *three* Mr Universes! So, congratulations to our three contestants, and thank you to our judges: Mrs Doris Higgins, Mrs Brenda Smith and Mrs Margaret Bottom. From all of us here, good night!

This sketch was first performed in 1983. The stage version is somewhat longer than that given here: we have omitted a number of visual jokes involving the painter's ladder, and a (mimed) electric door through which Bond and Barbara enter Mr Big's office, for example. Also, in the stage version, the sketch is followed by a song which is a pop video made by Hank. Our liking for misreadings of written texts – such as the book in Sketch 15 *The bus stop* (in Book 1) and the robber's note in Sketch 6 *The bank* (in this book) – recurs here in the badly typed film script.

Words and expressions

Connected with films:
producer, director, direct (vb.), *star* (n./vb.),
film (n./vb.), *script, title, scene, lines* (in the script),
play (vb.) (= play the part of)

Other expressions:
macaroni, cannelloni, pasta, secret agent, criminal (n.),
gun, shoot, paint (vb.), *paintbrush, ladder, typing
mistake, Go ahead* (= Yes, you can do what you
requested)

Preliminary practice

You could prepare for the sketch with a brief discussion about film styles, concerning what types of films the students like, the best film they have seen recently, etc., and then focus particularly on the James Bond series: Do the students like the Bond films, or do they agree, for example, with Hugh Grant's famous description of Bond as simply 'a boring 60s chauvinist with a bad toupee'?

If the social interaction in the class is very good, you could ask the students to nominate each other for particular roles in films, saying why they think their nominee would be suitable. (This is perhaps not a good activity for younger classes, where the students may take advantage of the situation to make fun of each other.)

Follow-up activities

① During the sketch, the characters rehearse part of a film script, which includes several typing mistakes: *eats* for *meets*, *Pond* for *Bond*, *Mr Pig* for *Mr Big*, *shout* for *shoot*, *Mr Bag* for *Mr Big*, and *rocket* for *pocket*. Here is an activity based on such mistakes.

In small groups, the students write some short dialogues. These dialogues can be of any type, but the students may like to imagine that they are extracts from film scripts; they do not need to be very long (ten lines is sufficient, for example). In their dialogues, the students make some 'typing mistakes' like those in the sketch, i.e. they replace a few words with other words.

Each group then passes their 'script' to another group. The groups then, in turn, act out the scripts they have received for the rest of the class to watch. They should act out the scripts exactly as they have received them, i.e. including the 'typing mistakes'. After each group has acted out a script, the rest of the class can identify and correct the 'typing mistakes'.

② For another activity in groups (or pairs), the students could write some telegrams, which they read out to the rest of the class. In reading them out, they can include the punctuation, saying *Stop* and *Comma* as in the sketch, if they like. The 'telegrams' could be instructions to other individuals in the class; e.g. Hello – *Comma* – Maria. *Stop*. Please stand up – *Comma* – turn round – *Comma* – and walk to the window. *Stop*.

Props and costumes

For classroom re-enacting, all that is really required is three 'film scripts' (it is useful to have the text of *Scene 6* written in them, including the typing mistakes), and a piece of paper to represent the telegram (with the telegram text written on it). The ladder, paint tin and paintbrush can be mimed.

For a performance, you will need the film scripts and the telegram, plus a real step-ladder, a paint tin – empty, so the painter is not obliged to deal with real paint – and a paintbrush. Hank could be sitting at a desk at the start, but this is not vital. Costumes: an overall for the painter; others as desired.

The new James Bond film

Scene   Hank Cannelloni's office

Characters   Hank Cannelloni, the director of the film

Linda Stone
Romeo Higgins } the stars of the film
A painter

Hank is in his office. There is a knock at the door.

Hank   Come in!

Linda comes in.

Linda   Hi, Hank!

Hank   Linda! Hi!

Linda   So, Hank, why do you want to see me?

Hank   Linda, I want you to be the star of my new film.

Linda   Great! Tell me about it.

Hank   I am going to direct the new James Bond film.

Linda   The new James Bond film!

Hank   Yes. It's going to be a great film – and you're going to be a big star!

Linda   I *am* a big star, Hank.

Hank   Yes, Linda, of course you're a big star. But you're going to be an even *bigger* star!

Linda   Great! Er…Hank…

Hank   Yes, Linda?

Linda   Who's going to play James Bond?

Hank   Well, we decided that we wanted Tom Cruise –

Linda   Tom Cruise?

Hank   Yes.

Linda   That's great!

Hank   But there's a small problem.

Linda   What's that, Hank?

Hank   Well –

There is a knock at the door.

Hank   Come in!

Romeo opens the door.

Romeo	Hello! Is anybody there?
Hank	Oh, hi, Romeo. Come in.
Romeo	Hello, Mr Macaroni.
Hank	Cannelloni.
Romeo	Cannelloni, yes. Sorry.
Hank	Romeo, come over here.
Romeo	Right. (*To Linda*) Oh, hello. I don't think we've met. I'm Romeo Higgins.
Linda	Romeo who?
Romeo	Higgins. H-I-G-
Linda	Hi, Romeo. (*To Hank, quietly*) Hank, who is Romeo Higgins?
Hank	(*To Linda, quietly*) He's…er…he's …
Romeo	I'm very pleased to meet you.
Linda	I'm sure you are.
Hank	Romeo is…er…starring in the film with you.
Linda	What?
Hank	Yes. He's going to be the new James Bond.
Linda	The new James Bond?
Romeo	Yes. I'm very excited about it.
Linda	(*To Hank, quietly*) What happened to Tom Cruise?
Hank	(*To Linda, quietly*) He's busy.
Linda	Oh, no!
Hank	OK, let's talk about the film. The film takes place in Honolulu.
Romeo	Great! Honolulu, Linda!
Hank	But we're not going to film it in Honolulu.
Linda	We're not going to film it in Honolulu?
Hank	No.
Linda	Where *are* we going to film it?
Hank	In Manchester.
Romeo	Great! My grandmother lives in Manchester. Er…Mr Macaroni?
Hank	Cannelloni! The name is Cannelloni!
Romeo	Oh, I can't tell the difference between macaroni and cannelloni.
Hank	What is it?
Romeo	Well, I know they're both types of pasta…
Hank	No, I mean: *What* do you *want*?
Romeo	Am I really going to be the new James Bond?
Hank	Yes, Romeo. Here's your script.

Hank gives Romeo a script.

Romeo	Oh, thank you.
Hank	And Linda…
Linda	Yes, Hank?
Hank	You play Barbara, another secret agent.

Hank gives Linda a script.

Linda	Thanks, Hank.

The painter enters with a ladder.

Painter	Is there anyone here called Macaroni?
Hank	Cannelloni! The name is Cannelloni!
Painter	Is that you?
Hank	Yes!
Painter	Telephone call for you, Mr Cannelloni.
Hank	Tell them I'm busy.
Painter	It's Hollywood.
Hank	Hollywood! Right – (***Starting to leave***) – I'll be back in a minute.
Painter	*Mr* Hollywood – your bank manager.
Hank	Ah. (***Coming back***) Right. Never mind.
Painter	Can I finish painting this wall?
Hank	Go ahead.

The painter sets up his ladder and starts painting.

Linda	Hank!
Hank	What is it, Linda?
Linda	I've just noticed the title of this film. It's called 'Bond Eats Mr Big'.
Painter	'Bond Eats Mr Big.' What a great title!
Hank	That's a typing mistake.
Romeo	A typing mistake?
Hank	Yes. It should be 'Bond *Meets* Mr Big'.
Romeo	Oh, yes – a typing mistake. There are hundreds of typing mistakes. The typing is really terrible. Who typed this rubbish?
Hank	I did.
Romeo	Oh.
Hank	Just do your best. Now, let's look at one of the important scenes. Scene 6 –

Hank, Linda and Romeo find Scene 6 in their scripts.

Hank	– where Bond –
Romeo	Yes.

Hank	– and Barbara –
Linda	Yes.
Hank	– go into the office of Mr Big.
Romeo	Mr Who?
Hank	Mr Big.
Romeo	Who's Mr Big?
Hank	He's the biggest, most dangerous criminal in the world.
Linda	Who's playing Mr Big in the film?
Hank	I am.

The painter laughs.

Hank	What's the matter with you?
Painter	(**Changing his laugh into a cough**) I've got a cold.
Hank	OK, remember: I'm Mr Big. So…lines, everybody.
Romeo	(**To Linda**) What did he say?
Linda	I don't know. (**To the painter**) What did he say?
Painter	I think he said 'lions'.

Romeo and Linda make the sound of lions roaring; the painter joins in.

Hank	I said *lines*, not *lions*!!
Romeo / **Linda**	Sorry, Hank.
Hank	OK, let's begin. (**Reading from his script, in a strange voice**) 'Ah-ha! Who are you?'
Linda	(**To Romeo**) What did he say?
Romeo	I don't know. (**To the painter**) What did he say?
Painter	'Who are you?'
Romeo	Romeo Higgins.
Painter	How do you do?
Romeo	How do you do?
Hank	Romeo! Lines! Just read the *lines*!
Romeo	What? Oh, yes. (**Reading**) 'My name is Pond – James Pond.'
Hank	What did you say?
Romeo	'My name is Pond – James Pond.'
Linda	It's not James *Pond*, it's James *Bond*! Idiot!
Romeo	(**Pointing at his script**) It says 'Pond' here.
Hank	Just get on with it! 'Ah-ha, Bond! This is the moment I've been waiting for!'
Romeo	(**To the painter**) What did he say?
Painter	I'm not sure, but I think he said: (**Imitating Hank's strange voice**) 'Ah-ha, Bond! This is the moment I've been waiting for!'

Romeo	Thanks.
Linda	'Look out, Bond! He's got a gun.'
Painter	No, I haven't. It's a paintbrush.
Romeo	'I'm not afraid of you, Mr Pig.'
Painter	Mr *Big*!
Romeo	'Mr Big.'
Linda	'Bond! Look out!'
Romeo	'What is it, Banana?' Er…'Barbara?'
Linda	'He's got a gun. He's going to shout!'
Painter	Not *'shout'* – *'shoot'*! 'He's going to *shoot*' – with his gun!
Romeo	'Don't shoot, Mr Bag!' – 'Mr *Big*!'
Hank	'Ah-ha! Why not!'
Romeo	'Because…'

Hank, Romeo and Linda all turn over a page in their scripts.

Romeo	'…I've got something I want to show you. It's here – in my rocket.'
Painter	Not *'rocket'* – *'pocket'*! 'It's here in my *pocket*.' Oh! Stop everything! I've got something I want to show you! It's here in my pocket!

The painter takes a telegram from his pocket.

Painter	It's a telegram for you, Mr Cannelloni – from the producer, Mr Broccoli.
Hank	From the producer?! Read it!
Painter	OK. (**Reading**) 'Hello. *Stop*. How are you? *Stop*. Have you started the film yet? *Stop*. If you've started – *Comma* – stop. *Stop*. If you haven't started – *Comma* – don't start. *Stop*. Stop. *Stop*. Signed: The Producer. *Stop*.'
Romeo	I didn't understand a word of that.
Linda	It means there's no film. (**Leaving**) Bye, Hank.
Hank	Er…Bye, Linda.
Romeo	No film?
Hank	That's right.
Romeo	Do you mean I'm not going to play James Bond?
Hank	I'm afraid not, Romeo.
Romeo	Oh, no! That means I haven't got a job.
Hank	*You* haven't got a job! What about *me*? I haven't got a job either!
Painter	Hank, Romeo, don't worry.
Hank	What do you mean?
Painter	I can give you both a job.
Romeo	Really?
Painter	Yes. Hank, you take this paintbrush…

He gives Hank his paintbrush.

Hank   What?

Painter   And Romeo, you take the ladder…

He gives Romeo his ladder.

Romeo   Eh?

Painter   Call me when you've finished. I'll be in the canteen.

The painter leaves.

16 World record

The idea for this sketch came from a role-playing activity devised by a member of the ETT to practise the Present Perfect Continuous tense with a class (the use of *How long have you been -ing…?* and *I've/He's/She's been -ing for [period of time]* seeming quite appropriate in the context of world record attempts). The students were filmed on video and very much enjoyed the activity. It was thus agreed that a sketch should be written for the show, based on the idea, and this sketch was the result. It was first performed in 1974.

Words and expressions

programme, studio, viewers, contestant, stand, lean (vb.), *break a record, bucket, brush* (n.), *trousers, look at, look for, have…on* (= wear), *take off*

The expression *…to go* occurs several times in the sketch, in sentences such as *You've got a long way to go!, You've only got four minutes to go!* and *Only ten seconds to go!*
Note the ironic tone of *Congratulations, Albert!*

Preliminary practice

The Guinness Book of Records contains some very unusual (often amazing) world records under the heading 'Human Achievements: Miscellaneous Endeavours'. Many of these involve strange activities, rather like those in the sketch.

If you can get hold of a copy of the book, you could select a few of these strange world records, such as walking with a milk bottle on one's head, playing the accordion non-stop, or sitting in a tree.

Write each activity (and the record distance, time, etc.) on a piece of paper and distribute the papers to the students. Each student mimes the activity on their paper, and the other students guess what it is. When it has been guessed correctly, the student who mimed it can tell the others the record distance, time, and so on.

Follow-up activities

① The students may like to do another version of the sketch, in which Albert and Mabel are trying to break different world records. Here are some suggestions (the students may have ideas of their own, of course):

Sitting on top of a flagpole.
Walking from one end of the country to another.
Eating eggs.
Telling jokes non-stop.

② In the sketch, Albert's world record attempt fails, but the students could imagine an alternative ending in which he is successful and holds a press conference. Four students could sit at the front of the class in the roles of the four 'celebrities': Albert, Mrs Hargreaves, Michael Moonshine and Mabel Phillips. The rest of the class are journalists asking questions. The journalists could be in four groups, with each group being designated to put questions to a particular person, so that not all the questions are put to Albert.

③ During the 'press conference' activity, the students playing the journalists could take notes of the celebrities' answers. Then the celebrities could join the relevant groups, and the groups could each produce a short newspaper article, entitled *A New World Record: 'My Story' by Albert Hargreaves* (or *…by Daisy Hargreaves, …by Michael Moonshine, …by Mabel Phillips*).

Props and costumes

For classroom re-enacting, a pen or pencil or rolled paper can represent a microphone, held by Michael; Mabel can lean on anything (a desk, for example); Albert can mime standing in the bucket.

For a more elaborate performance, a real microphone is useful (although it does not have to be plugged in), and you will need a long-handled brush or broom for Mabel, a bucket for Albert and a jug for Mrs Hargreaves. It is best if the bucket and jug are empty, i.e. Mrs Hargreaves *pretends* to pour soup into the bucket. Michael and Mrs Hargreaves should have watches to consult. Costumes: Michael could have a shiny TV-presenter's jacket or suit; costumes for the other characters as desired.

World record

Scene A TV studio
Characters Michael Moonshine
Albert Hargreaves
Daisy Hargreaves, Albert's wife
Mabel Phillips
A man

Michael Thank you, thank you, thank you. Yes, ladies and gentlemen, this is the programme that gives *you* the chance to break a world record. We have here in the studio tonight two people who are trying to break world records. Let's meet them and see what they're doing. Tell me, sir, what is your name?

Albert Albert Hargreaves.

Michael Albert Hargreaves. Well, Albert, what are you doing?

Albert I'm standing on one leg in a bucket of hot soup.

Michael Ladies and gentlemen, he's standing on one leg in a bucket of hot soup!

The audience applauds.

Michael Albert, how long have you been standing on one leg in that bucket of hot soup?

Albert I've been standing here for six hours and fifty-eight minutes.

Michael And what is the world record for standing on one leg in a bucket of hot soup?

Albert The world record is seven hours and three minutes, Michael.

Michael Seven hours and three minutes! And you've been standing there for *six* hours and *fifty-nine* minutes now. Well, Albert, you've only got *four* minutes to go!

The audience applauds.

Michael Albert, you've been standing on one leg in that bucket of soup for almost seven hours now.

Albert That's right, Michael.

Michael Tell me – is the soup still hot?

Albert Yes. My wife's been coming in every half-hour with more hot soup. Here she comes now.

Mrs Hargreaves comes in.

Daisy Here you are, Albert.

She pours some hot soup into the bucket.

Albert Aaaargh!

Michael Well, I'm glad it's *your* leg in the soup, Albert, and not mine.

The audience laughs.

Michael   Now we have another contestant in the studio, a very charming young lady. Can you tell the viewers your name?

Mabel   Mabel Phillips.

Michael   Mabel Phillips. Well, Mabel, what are *you* doing?

Mabel   I'm leaning on this brush.

Michael   She's leaning on a brush, ladies and gentlemen!

The audience applauds.

Michael   Mabel, how long have you been leaning on that brush?

Mabel   I've been leaning on this brush for three hours and seventeen minutes.

Michael   She's been leaning on the brush for three hours and seventeen minutes. What is the world record for leaning on a brush, Mabel?

Mabel   Thirty-seven hours and fifty-six minutes.

Michael   Thirty-seven hours and fifty-six minutes! And you've been leaning on that brush for three hours and seventeen minutes. Well, Mabel, you've got…three, four, five, six – you've got a long way to go!

The audience laughs.

Michael   Well, Albert has been standing on one leg in his bucket of hot soup for *seven* hours and *one* minute, so he's only got *two* more minutes to go! Poor Mabel's got a *long* way to go…And here is another young man – and he hasn't got any trousers on.

The audience laughs.

Michael   Now, sir, what are *you* doing?

Man   I'm looking for my trousers.

Michael   I can see that. And how *long* have you been looking for your trousers?

Man   I've been looking for my trousers for five minutes.

Michael   And what's the world record?

Man   Pardon?

Michael   What's the world record for looking for trousers?

Man   I'm not trying to break a world record. I took my trousers off to have a bath, and when I got out of the bath, my trousers were gone.

Michael   I see. Get out of the way! We're on television!

The audience laughs.

Michael   Sorry about that, ladies and gentlemen. Now back to Albert Hargreaves. Albert, you've been standing in that bucket of hot soup for seven hours and *two* minutes. Only *one* more minute to go, and you will break the world record. And here comes Mrs Hargreaves with more hot soup!

Daisy   Here you are, Albert.

She pours some more soup into the bucket.

Albert   Aaaargh!

Michael   Tell me, Albert, how does it feel?

Albert   Hot!

The audience laughs.

Michael   No, no, no! How does it feel to be approaching the world record?

Albert   Well, Michael, I've been dreaming about this moment, I've been thinking about nothing else –

Michael   Yes, Albert.

Albert   – I've been practising every day –

Michael   Yes, Albert.

Albert   *Twice* on Sundays!

Michael   Yes – and here comes Mrs Hargreaves.

Albert   Oh no, not again!

Michael   It's all right, Albert, she's only looking at her watch!

The audience laughs.

Daisy   Albert! Albert! Only ten seconds to go! Ten, nine, eight, seven –

Mabel pushes Albert.

Mabel   (**Ironically**) Congratulations, Albert!

Albert   Aaaargh!

Albert falls over.

Michael   Well, ladies and gentlemen, Albert Hargreaves *hasn't* broken a world record, but he *has* broken…his leg!!

Notes and reminders

Notes and reminders

Notes and reminders

Notes and reminders

English Sketches Questionnaire

We are committed to continuing research into materials development. We would be very interested to hear your feedback about this resource book. Please photocopy this form and send it to your local Macmillan office or to the address at the bottom of the form. Thank you for your help.

Name:..

Name of school:..

Address of school:...

Average age of students:.......................................

Size of class:..

Frequency and length of lesson:...........................

Course materials currently used with class:

....

....

Supplementary materials currently used with class:

....

....

Please tell us if you have enjoyed using this photocopiable teacher's resource book. If not, please tell us why not; if you have, please tell us why.

....

....

....

What features do you like most about this resource book? What do you like least?

....

....

....

Do you have any suggestions for improvements?

....

....

....

What other kinds of materials would you like to see in a photocopiable format?

....

....

....

Please check the boxes below if you would like information about new materials or would like to help us in materials development.

I would like to receive information about new materials for ...

☐ children   ☐ adults

☐ exams   ☐ readers

☐ secondary school students

☐ university students

☐ business English

☐ supplementary materials

Would you be willing to help us develop new materials to suit your needs? Yes, I would like to ...

☐ pilot materials in my classroom.

☐ answer questionnaires.

☐ discuss my needs with a Macmillan Representative.

Please return this form to:
Editor, Macmillan Oxford, 4 Between Towns Road, Cowley, Oxford OX4 3PP.
If you would prefer to fax the form, please send to +44 1865 405799